SIR JOHN FRANKLIN

Expeditions to Destiny

ANTHONY DALTON

HERITAGE

VICTORIA · VANCOUVER · CALGARY

Heritage House Publishing Company Ltd.
heritagehouse.ca

Library and Archives Canada Cataloguing in Publication
Dalton, Anthony, 1940–
    Sir John Franklin: expeditions to destiny / Anthony Dalton.

(Amazing stories)
Includes bibliographical references and index.
Issued also in electronic format.
ISBN 978-1-927051-81-8

    1. Franklin, John, Sir, 1786-1847. 2. Explorers—Great Britain—Biography. 3. Arctic regions—Discovery and exploration—British. 4. Northwest Passage—Discovery and exploration—British. I. Title.

FC3961.1.F73D35 2012   917.1904'1092   C2012-904120-3

Series editor: Lesley Reynolds
Proofreader: Liesbeth Leatherbarrow

Cover photo: Sir John Franklin, QO221, The Mariners' Museum, Newport News, VA, USA

The interior of this book was produced on 100% post-consumer recycled paper, processed chlorine free and printed with vegetable-based inks.

Heritage House acknowledges the financial support for its publishing program from the Government of Canada through the Canada Book Fund (CBF), Canada Council for the Arts and the province of British Columbia through the British Columbia Arts Council and the Book Publishing Tax Credit.

 Canadian Heritage / Patrimoine canadien   Canada Council for the Arts / Conseil des Arts du Canada   BRITISH COLUMBIA ARTS COUNCIL

16 15 14 13 12 1 2 3 4 5

Printed in Canada

In memory of Keith Waterman

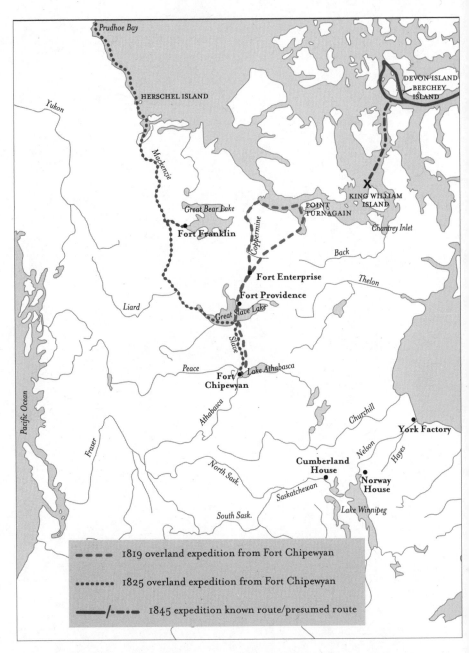

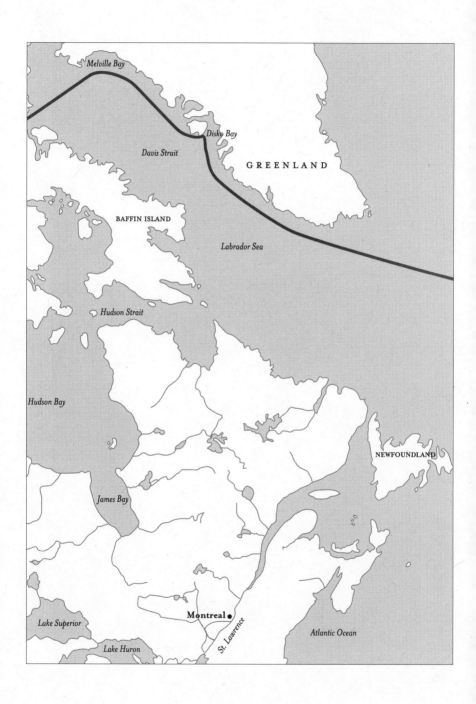

Melville Bay

Disko Bay

Davis Strait

GREENLAND

BAFFIN ISLAND

Labrador Sea

Hudson Strait

Hudson Bay

NEWFOUNDLAND

James Bay

Lake Superior

Montreal •

St. Lawrence

Atlantic Ocean

Lake Huron

Polar exploration is at once the cleanest and most isolated way of having a bad time which has been devised.

—APSLEY CHERRY-GARRARD,
THE WORST JOURNEY IN THE WORLD

Contents

SIR JOHN FRANKLIN CAPT.ᴺ R.N.

Prologue

THE SHIP WAS BARELY VISIBLE *in the almost whiteout conditions: the Arctic world clad in winter dressing. Thick snow covered everything with a freezing mantle. For five days without a break, a late blizzard had raged across King William Island and the adjoining ice-covered channels and straits. The vicious, unrelenting wind drove the snow before it in close-packed horizontal sheets. The sea ice groaned under the wind's onslaught and moved with a restless, erratic rhythm. When the pressure of ice on ice became too much, large blocks launched themselves up and away from the pack with a thunderous rumble, only to settle again at a different angle. With each crash, loud even above the wind's howl, the ship shuddered and whined, as if in fear. It was a time for all* creatures, sailors included, to lie dormant wherever shelter could be found.

Close at hand, hidden behind the ghostlike outline of the stunted masts and stubby hull stood another ship, almost identical in appearance. One of the two, the flagship, carried the name Erebus; the more distant was her consort, Terror. The two exploration ships of Britain's Royal Navy had been trapped in the same field of thick ice just off the bleak north-west coastline of King William Island for nearly a year, since the late summer of 1846. The winter that followed and led into 1847 had been harsh, and spring had never shown its smiling face.

There was no sign of life on either of the vessels, but they were far from empty. Huddled in the relative warmth below decks, the crews alternated between work and rest, just as they would on a normal day at sea. The walls and decks dripped with damp, the incipient ice only held at bay by the coal-burning fire amidships and another in the stern. In the master's cabin on HMS Erebus, the expedition's commander, Sir John Franklin, lay on his bed wrapped in blankets. Standing close by was his second-in-command, Captain Francis Crozier, and the ship's surgeon, Stephen Stanley. At the door stood Captain James Fitzjames. Crozier and Fitzjames were dressed in ill-fitting officer's uniforms that showed signs of hard wear, thin woollen blankets wrapped around their shoulders. The surgeon, dressed in similar fashion, leaned over his commanding officer, wiping the sick man's face with a damp cloth.

Prologue

The little that could be seen of Franklin showed he was just a shadow of his former robust self. The pile of blankets covered an emaciated replica of a once vigorous and proud man. His eyes were closed, his face as white as the snow and ice that had held the ship fast for so many months. His sunken cheeks showed his suffering.

Crozier's face was a mask. He stood beside the surgeon, studying the expedition's commander for a few minutes and then shook his head. Without a word he left the cabin, ushering his fellow officer ahead of him. Outside, he paused and said, "James, I fear for Sir John's life. Every hour he gets weaker."

Sir John Franklin, known to some as "the Lion of the Arctic," was 61 years old. He had fallen ill suddenly a few days before, perhaps from the same deadly malady that had affected some of his crew. His condition worsened by the hour. Franklin's enormous energy was exhausted. His final adventure had almost reached its end. The days passed— an endless succession of unchanging hours. Sir John Franklin fought to hold on to the last threads of his historic life. The cold gripped the trapped ships in a deathly vice as fuel and food supplies became more and more depleted. For Franklin, and for many of his officers and men on the two ships, there would be no escape from the sickness that attacked them. There would be no escape from the dreadful ice that surrounded their Arctic world. They all would spend eternity in unmarked, frozen Arctic graves.

Introduction

VIKING SAILORS KNEW THE SUBARCTIC seas well. They crossed the Atlantic between the 11th and 15th centuries to set up colonies in Iceland and Greenland, and also travelled farther west to Newfoundland and Labrador and north into what is now Baffin Bay. There is no evidence, however, that they ventured beyond there to seek a westerly route to Asia through the ice-choked islands. A few centuries before the Vikings, intrepid Irish monks had also braved the North Atlantic in their quest for new lands and peoples. Although they went ashore in Iceland, like the Vikings who were yet to come, they did not venture farther north into the icy realms of the Arctic.

In spite of those early expeditionary voyages across the

Introduction

North Atlantic, the American continent was unknown to most European nations until 1492, when Christopher Columbus reached its eastern shores. Before then, visionaries though they certainly were, curious men such as Columbus and John Cabot had not dreamed of an unknown continent on the other side of the North Atlantic. They were convinced that Asia lay on the west side of the vast ocean that washed Europe's shores.

After Columbus proved the existence of a large land mass standing between the Atlantic and Pacific Oceans, new routes to Asia had to be considered. John Cabot led the first known expedition that attempted to traverse the Arctic route across North America to China, setting sail from England in May 1498 with five ships to search for a short sea route to the riches of the east. One of the five ships limped into an Irish port in July of that year. The other four and their crews, including Cabot, were never seen again.

Yorkshire-born Martin Frobisher, a former pirate, followed John Cabot in 1576. He reached the east coast of Baffin Island and returned to England just four months after he left. Some of the indigenous rocks he carried home were thought to contain gold. Frobisher went back to the Baffin coast in 1577 with three ships to collect more. When he returned, the "gold" was found to be nothing more valuable than iron pyrites. Frobisher led another expedition to the region the following year and forced his way deep into

Hudson Strait. Adverse weather conditions sent him home again in September that year.

After Frobisher's failure to find the elusive waterway through the Arctic, a long list of now-illustrious British explorers made their own attempts. They included the Devonshire navigator and brilliant seaman John Davis, and the ill-fated Henry Hudson, who was followed by Thomas Button, William Baffin, Robert Bylot, Luke Foxe, Thomas James, the famed James Cook, John Ross, James Clark Ross, William Parry, and in 1818, Lieutenant John Franklin, who was sent on an expeditionary voyage to the North Pole and an attempt to find the Northwest Passage.

Franklin stands out among these bold explorers, living on in history as "the man who ate his boots" and as the leader of a large expedition that disappeared in the Arctic in 1846. Sir John Franklin was a complex, intelligent man—and a strong but gentle leader—who spent much of his life as a Royal Navy officer, often at sea, plus a few years on arduous overland expeditions to the Arctic. He was also considered unlucky, a reference to his diplomatic and expedition failures and the men he lost in the field.

When Franklin and his crew of 129 men and two ships vanished in the Arctic in 1845, the search for the expedition, or evidence of its fate, became one of the most exhaustive quests of the 19th century. For years after, naval ships and private expeditions set out for the ice to search for clues to the whereabouts of the ships and men. Franklin's devoted second wife, Jane, was instrumental in orchestrating much of the effort to find answers. She spent a large part of her personal fortune over several years without any success in finding her husband or any of his men alive.

Sir John Franklin's enigmatic story, with the loss of so many men on a single expedition, has fascinated historians for decades. It continues to lure adventurers to the Canadian Arctic and to excite armchair explorers to this day.

CHAPTER

1

The Boy Sailor

THE ENGLISH COUNTY OF LINCOLNSHIRE is mostly flat, and thanks to the less than perfect climate, it is often damp. There are a few rolling hills, but nothing more imposing than about 131 feet (40 metres) above sea level. There are protective man-made dykes close to the coast and, ranging in from there, large tracts of land devoid of trees. In some ways, it is reminiscent of the North Sea it borders.

John Franklin, who would one day become known as one of the greatest Arctic explorers, was born on this damp Lincolnshire land in the middle of April 1786. He hailed from a small town named Spilsby and went to the local school with Alfred Tennyson, destined eventually to be acclaimed as one of Britain's finest poets. The young John Franklin was described by Tennyson as "a chubby cherub, round-faced and round-headed." It was, perhaps, an apt description. Most of those features remained with him throughout his life. The son of a prominent businessman, Franklin had seven sisters and an older brother.

Franklin's first sight of the sea at the Lincolnshire coast is said to have laid the groundwork for the rest of his life. Although only a boy, he determined to sail the world's oceans and talked his father into getting him a job on a small freighter operating between nearby Hull, on England's east coast, and Lisbon, the Portuguese capital. By the end of his first voyage, Franklin knew he wanted to spend his life at sea. At the age of 14, he joined the Royal Navy with the lowly rank of first-class volunteer. Presumably that meant he had to work without pay for a while.

The enthusiastic young sailor was assigned to HMS *Polyphemus*, under the command of Captain John Lawford, and in March 1801, he set sail for the Baltic Sea and into the Battle of Copenhagen. Second in command of the British fleet at that brief war was the great naval hero Lord Horatio Nelson, then Vice-Admiral, who would later die at Trafalgar. The battle was fought in the straits between Sweden and Denmark and within sight of Kronborg Castle, the setting for William Shakespeare's epic play *Hamlet*. Young John Franklin survived his first action against enemy forces without injury and returned to England safely that summer. Thanks to his father's influence and his own persistence, he was transferred to HMS *Investigator* as a midshipman under famed explorer Captain Matthew Flinders. Franklin was perhaps fortunate that Captain Flinders was another Lincolnshire man and also a distant relative.

Investigator, an old and tired ship, was bound for the other side of the world. Flinders's orders were to circumnavigate New Holland, now known as Australia, and to complete a survey of the coastline. The ship sailed away from England at the end of the first week in July 1801 with an excited Midshipman Franklin on board. He would not see his homeland or his family again for just over three years. As a "middy," Franklin was classed as a junior officer but still had to sleep in a hammock between decks like an ordinary seaman.

Charged with surveying and scientific duties for the voyage, John Franklin soon made himself popular with Flinders and with his fellow officers. He worked and studied hard and showed a natural ability for making precise astronomical observations. Having Matthew Flinders as a mentor and instructor must have been of huge benefit to the young Franklin's education. An added bonus for Franklin was the presence on board of naturalist Robert Brown; the two young men would become firm friends.

The long voyage to the other side of the world was distinguished by two remarkable and tragic events: one of the younger officers and seven men under his command were lost from a small boat close to the Australian coast, and the venerable *Investigator* was found to be leaking like a sieve and constantly in danger of sinking. But despite the ship's unseaworthy condition, Flinders, a master mariner, completed his circumnavigation and made it into Sydney 11 months after leaving England. That was as far as *Investigator* would go. Unfit for further service at sea, she was condemned to end her days in the harbour as a storage hulk.

With the officers and crew as far away from home as they could possibly be, transport back to England had to be arranged. Captain Flinders, Midshipman John Franklin and a portion of *Investigator's* crew took passage on board HMS *Porpoise* in August 1803. The naval ship was to travel in convoy with two merchantmen, *Cato* and *Bridgewater*. The voyage was a disaster. Six days into the journey, on August 17, *Porpoise* and *Cato* ran up onto an uncharted reef off Australia's northeast coast at dusk and were wrecked. *Bridgewater*, perhaps unaware of the calamity, continued on into the gathering darkness of evening. Her own destiny was not far away. She called at a port in the Dutch East Indies before disappearing forever.

Franklin, still only a teenager, had experienced his first shipwreck with the sudden demise of HMS *Porpoise*. He was among 94 officers and men who survived the accident and fetched up on a bank of coral and sand only 900 feet long by 50 feet wide (274 by 15 metres). Flinders named the piece of land Wreck Reef, for obvious reasons. Part of the Great Barrier Reef, it bears that name to this day.

Fortunately for Flinders, Franklin and the remainder of the castaways, a six-oared cutter had somehow escaped unscathed. Flinders and a handful of men embarked on an epic 700-mile (1,127-kilometre) voyage in the small open boat for Sydney, and they made it. It is one of the great small-boat journeys in exploration history. Franklin and the others, meanwhile, had to camp out on the prominent but barren reef and wait for rescue. They did so with good humour, using canvas tents for shelter, and erected a flag pole with an inverted flag to signal their distress.

When Flinders returned for the shipwrecked sailors with three ships, Midshipman Franklin was sent on the first stage of a long voyage home. He boarded the merchantman *Rolla*, bound for Canton on the south China coast. From there he joined an Indiaman, *Earl Camden*, one of a fleet of 16 or more merchant ships outbound for England under the command of Commodore Nathaniel Dance of the Honourable East India Company. In mid-February 1804, at the entrance to the Malacca Straits, the lightly armed British ships came under attack by a French naval force of five heavily armed ships led by famed Contre-Admiral Charles-Alexandre Léon Durand, Comte de Linois.

The French war fleet consisted of a 74-gun battle ship, *Marengo*; two frigates, the 40-gun *Belle Poule* and the 36-gun *Sémillante*; plus two corvettes carrying 38 guns between them. Against all odds, Dance's fleet routed the Frenchmen and continued their voyage. Although there were deaths in the brief fight, Franklin again came through the action unscathed. He reached his home shores in August 1804. He was then 18 years old and a veteran sailor with a long list of adventures behind him, including two sea battles. Much more was to come for the Lincolnshire lad.

During the Napoleonic Wars, Midshipman Franklin served on HMS *Bellerophon* at the blockade of Brest in 1805, a monotonous duty designed to prevent the French fleet from sailing, and which achieved little else. He was also on *Bellerophon* at the much more exciting Battle of Trafalgar on October 21, 1805. In that epic battle, 32 British warships took on the combined might of the French and Spanish navies off southern Spain's Cape Trafalgar, just to the south of Cadiz.

The British fleet fought in two squadrons, the windward led by Admiral Lord Nelson in HMS *Victory* and the leeward commanded by Vice-Admiral Collingwood in HMS *Royal Sovereign*. *Victory* and *Royal Sovereign*, out in front of their two squadrons, bore the brunt of the fire from the wide and powerful French and Spanish line. *Bellerophon*, with Franklin on board, was not far away. She was part of the leeward squadron, located four ships to the west of *Royal Sovereign* at the beginning of the fray.

When Admiral Lord Nelson sent his famous signal that morning, "England expects that every man will do his duty," Franklin would have cheered with the rest of the British sailors. He willingly took part in the fight that became

Admiral Nelson's flagship, HMS *Victory*, is on permanent display at Portsmouth, England. Franklin served on HMS *Bellerophon*, a similar style of ship, which fought beside *Victory* at the Battle of Trafalgar. ANTHONY DALTON

an overwhelming victory for Nelson's fleet. Admiral Nelson, perhaps the greatest naval commander of all time, did not survive the battle. Never one to shy away from danger, he commanded his ship in full military regalia—a tempting target for a determined sharpshooter. Nelson was hit by a musket ball in the heat of the battle and thrown to the deck, breaking his back. He died in a berth below decks soon after, in the arms of his most trusted officers.

On *Bellerophon*, the number of dead and wounded climbed swiftly as the battle progressed. The ship's master, Captain John Cooke, was killed in the early afternoon. On the poop deck, where Franklin served, a fellow midshipman standing beside him was also killed. Of the 40 fighting men on that deck, only 8 survived that violent day; among the fortunate few was John Franklin. Over 1,500 British seamen and thousands of French and Spanish sailors died at Trafalgar. Franklin fought, as he had done in previous engagements, but did not distinguish himself. He appears to have been lucky in battle. He had a few close calls from musket balls, grapeshot and flying splinters but came through the firestorm without so much as a scratch, although the overwhelming noise of the battle affected his hearing for the rest of his life.

With his service at the Battle of Trafalgar now on his navy record, Midshipman John Franklin was promoted to master's mate in 1807 and sent to serve aboard HMS *Bedford*. Two months later, he was promoted to acting lieutenant and went from war to escort duty. For his first voyage in that ship, he had the honour of helping take the Portuguese royal family to exile in Brazil, and he remained in Rio de Janeiro at the beck and call of the Portuguese royals for the next two years. It was not an exacting duty, and it was certainly safer than fighting a war, but it lacked the action that Franklin craved.

While Franklin languished in diplomatic comfort in

Rio de Janeiro, Britain was at war again, this time with another close neighbour—Holland. Soon after *Bedford*'s return to England, the fighting ship, with Lieutenant Franklin aboard, took part in the blockade of Holland's Texel River.

Franklin and *Bedford* subsequently fought in the British-American war of 1812–14, both being involved in an attack on New Orleans. While on duty in that conflict, Franklin suffered a non–life-threatening wound in his shoulder. At the time, he was in command of the ship's boats in a brief fight against American gunboats. His actions were successful enough that he was mentioned in dispatches and received a medal for his pains. HMS *Bedford* arrived home in 1815. Soon after, Franklin was promoted to first lieutenant and assigned to HMS *Forth* as second-in-command. His next custodial errand was a short voyage across the Channel to escort the Duchess of Angoulême home to France from exile in England.

In September of that year, with peace on the seas and no immediate need for a large fleet of ships and men, the Royal Navy began to shed its expensive roster of both. Along with hundreds of others, Franklin was paid off. With nothing useful to do with his time, he watched the idle days stretch into weeks. The weeks became a year, then two, then the beginning of a third. He began to wonder if he would ever get back to sea.

The only brightness on Franklin's somewhat gloomy

horizon at this tedious time was his friendship with
Robert Brown, the naturalist from the Australian voyage. Brown had important friends, in particular Sir Joseph
Banks, president of the Royal Society. Banks was a man
who wielded great political power, although he was in his
sixties and restricted to a wheelchair. He had an impressive background in exploration and was also a renowned
botanist. Among his credits was a circumnavigation
of the world with the celebrated Captain James Cook.
Franklin wanted to get back to sea, and he wanted to
be involved in more explorations. He needed someone
like the president of the Royal Society on his side. Robert
Brown offered to put Franklin's name in front of Banks.

For almost a decade, another man had been courting
Banks' favour. He had become accustomed to spending an
evening each week discussing exploration with the old sci-
entist. His name was John Barrow. He would become one of
the most influential British figures in 19th-century exploration planning on sea and on land and would figure largely
in John Franklin's life.

CHAPTER

2

To the Arctic

WHILE FRANKLIN FRETTED OVER HIS lack of employment at home in Lincolnshire, John Barrow—friend to the eminent Sir Joseph Banks—was gradually making his mark at the Admiralty in London. Since 1804 he had been a lowly yet ambitious second secretary with a passion for geography and exploration. In Barrow's time the Second Secretary to the Admiralty was a civil servant. His superior, the First Secretary, was a member of the British government.

John Barrow was born on farmland in Lancashire in 1764. By his tenth birthday it was obvious to anyone who cared to notice that the boy possessed a quick and agile mind. At 13 he was fluent enough in Latin and Greek to read and write the languages. By the time he reached the age of 20, he had added mathematics and astronomy to his skills and had spent one summer on a whaling voyage in the icy waters around Spitsbergen, giving him valuable experience for the future.

Barrow's remarkable intelligence gave him occasional introductions to influential people. While tutoring a child prodigy, the son of a baronet, he learned Chinese—from the boy. That accomplishment, added to the baronet's contacts, landed Barrow a job as interpreter to a British diplomatic mission to China under Lord Macartney in 1795. The mission was not a success, but Macartney took note of Barrow's abilities. When Macartney was sent to South Africa as governor of the Cape Colony a few months later, he took Barrow with him. During the next few years in Africa, Barrow explored and mapped much of the territory as far north as the Orange River. He married the daughter of a Cape Colony judge, and his work earned him the respect of additional potential patrons. He and his family returned to England in 1803, and his carefully collected contacts placed him in the Admiralty in 1804. By then he had had two books published, one on China and the other on Africa, and was recognized by his peers as a geographer and a cartographer.

By 1816, Barrow had developed enough political clout in the Admiralty and with the Royal Society to make decisions as to where his country should send expeditions. As a result, British expeditions went to West Africa to determine the direction of the Niger River and to try to reach the fabled city of Timbuktu. They also went to the Congo. In 1817, Barrow began planning an Arctic expedition to search for the Northwest Passage. Thanks to John Barrow's effective arguments, the Royal Navy had been persuaded to use its ships and crews, in peacetime, to further England's knowledge of the world. Early in 1818, he received permission to mount his Arctic expedition.

That spring, after two and a half tedious years cooling his heels on land waiting for orders to join a ship, Lieutenant Franklin's friendship with notable people, such as the eminent naturalist Robert Brown, paid off. Like John Barrow, Brown was a friend of Sir Joseph Banks, a powerful figure in exploration politics. Brown's influence extended to the Admiralty, where Barrow spent his working days, and as a result, Franklin received welcome news. In spite of stiff competition from other officers, also stumbling along on limited pay, he had been selected to take command of the 250-ton brig HMS *Trent* as part of a four-ship expedition into the Arctic.

Two naval ships would set course for Baffin Bay; the other two—Franklin's half of the venture—would sail straight north in an attempt to conquer the ice and reach the North Pole. For this mission, *Trent* would sail in convoy with the 370-ton HMS *Dorothea*, commanded by Captain David Buchan, the leader of this part of the expedition.

The ambitious orders for Buchan and Franklin were written by John Barrow in his Admiralty capacity and read in part: "Although it is highly desirable in the interest of science and the extension of natural knowledge that you should reach the Pole, yet that passage between the Atlantic and the Pacific is the main object of your mission." At the same time, Captain John Ross and Lieutenant William Edward Parry were ordered to explore Baffin Bay in the chartered whaler *Isabella* and the specially strengthened *Alexander*. In fact, Franklin and his three fellow navy officers were being sent on a two-pronged mission to search for a Northwest Passage. The Baffin Bay expedition had far more chance of success, while a navigable route over the North Pole had to be an unlikely possibility; even so, Franklin was elated at this opportunity. His long Arctic career, which would be interrupted a few times, was about to begin.

Trent and *Dorothea* sailed out of the Thames estuary on April 25. A few hours into the voyage, *Trent* was already showing signs of leaking—not a good omen for a rough sea journey to the Far North. After a stop to enlist additional crew at Lerwick, in the Shetland Islands, the two ships set course almost due north to Spitsbergen and the edge of the polar ice pack. En route, *Trent*'s leak became worse and threatened the safety of the ship. The cause was eventually found to be a hole in the hull, below the waterline, where a large iron bolt should have been. The hole had been filled in and disguised with tar and pitch. The jet of icy water that blasted in was said to be all of 4 feet (1.2 metres) high.

Close to the pack ice off Spitsbergen's west coast, officers and crews of both ships delighted in the sights of seals, sea lions, walrus and occasional whales, plus the aggressive antics of polar bears patrolling the ice and the surrounding sea. The marine creatures were fascinating, but the Arctic weather gave much cause for concern. Furious gales coated the ships with ice, from the hulls to their topmasts. Crews had to be employed for hours at a time hacking ice away from the decks and bows, and beating thick ice off the rigging. Without that regular effort, the ships would have become top-heavy and capsized.

When the weather cleared enough to see long distances to the north, the officers and crews of both ships saw ice "in one vast unbroken plain," stretching all the way to the horizon. They were looking at brash ice (large fragments of broken ice drifting together), about 5 feet (1.5 metres) thick, spreading out from the heavier pack ice. It looked impenetrable, but upon close inspection by Franklin in *Trent*, it proved to have a few narrow leads, or avenues of open water. Franklin forced *Trent* into the ice by ramming his reinforced bow against the floes and soon found himself frozen in for a night. With daylight came a slight thaw, enough for *Trent* to be worked free again and force her way back to the open sea, where her sister ship waited.

Off the northwest extremity of the archipelago on June 12, both ships became trapped in thick ice and suffered damage. They remained there, incapable of moving in any direction, until a lead opened on July 6 and they were able to steer clear of the pack for a while. They were soon surrounded again, and when all else failed, Buchan managed to keep his ships moving north into the pack ice by warping them forward. That entailed running out an anchor, embedding it in ice and then winching the ship up to it. It was a slow process that endangered the ships and tired the crews. Even worse, sometimes the crews had to drag the ships themselves. Conditions became so bad by July 19 that Buchan was considering aborting the northern route to the pole in favour of an attempt to the west.

The ice began to freeze behind them, closing off their escape route. Buchan recognized the peril of being held fast in the ice pack and set about getting both ships warped to safety. It took nearly 10 days to cover the 30 miles (48 kilometres) to open water. After enormous physical effort by the crews, they worked free, but they had lost a lot of ground. As the two ships fought clear of the frozen dangers, the wind made up Buchan's mind about the direction they would travel.

By this time the two ships were in drift ice off the east coast of Greenland. A violent gale drove them hard toward the polar pack again. A report written by Lieutenant Frederick Beechey, Franklin's first officer, described the danger to *Trent*: "The vessel staggered under the shock and for a moment seemed to recoil; but the next wave, curling up under her counter, drove her about her own length within the margin of the ice, where she gave one roll, and was immediately thrown broadside to the wind by the succeeding wave."

Beechey continued his story with a blatant compliment aimed at his captain, John Franklin: "I will not conceal the pride I felt in witnessing the bold and decisive tone in which the orders were issued by the commander of our little vessel and the promptitude and steadiness with which they were executed by the crew." In the years to come, Lieutenant Beechey would go on to build his own claim to Arctic fame.

By the end of August, once the two ships had been worked clear of the polar pack and found a modicum of safety at Fairhaven on Spitsbergen's north coast, it was obvious that *Dorothea* was too badly damaged to continue the Arctic voyage. As the expedition's commander, Captain Buchan ordered his charges turned for home, despite Franklin's request for *Trent* to be allowed to continue alone. They limped south together and arrived on the Thames on October 22.

Franklin was disappointed at the early termination of the expedition, but he had learned valuable lessons about Arctic navigation and how to work ships through drifting ice. Although Franklin and Buchan had not realized any of their objectives, their half of the Arctic expedition was looked upon with approval because of a series of scientific discoveries they had made, albeit inadvertently. While checking depth soundings in 300 fathoms (548 metres) of water, the lead brought up a section of coral, as well as living starfish (*Ophiocoma echinata*) and rare sea worms (*Glycera unicornis*), one of which was "caught between the ship's [HMS *Trent's*] side and the edge of a large flow of ice." They also brought up lobsters. The coral find was significant because it only thrives in warm water. Its presence in the icy waters of the Far North immediately prompted a series of questions: How did it get to the Arctic? Was the Arctic once warm enough for coral to grow in its vastness? What other mysteries might scientists uncover in the Arctic waters? Buchan and Franklin left such intellectual musings to the scientists in their warm laboratories. Their own interests were in further exploring the North.

Ross and Parry returned to England from Baffin Bay in December after failing to find an entrance to the Northwest Passage. In their defence, however, they had been more successful than Buchan and Franklin. They had charted previously unmapped coastlines on Baffin Bay and had had useful discourse with the indigenous Inuit people—the Eskimos, as they were known at the time.

Among those who served on the four ships of this expedition was an impressive lineup of naval officers who would make their names in Arctic exploration over the next three decades. They included Captain John Ross and his nephew, Midshipman James Clark Ross, plus Lieutenant William Parry, Captain David Buchan, Lieutenant Frederick W. Beechey, Midshipman George Back, and of course, the determined Lieutenant John Franklin.

CHAPTER

3

Rivers, Muskeg and Waterfalls

WHILE NEITHER OF THE TWO Arctic expeditions of 1818 had been successful in attaining their goals, they had brought back some useful information. As a result, Barrow sent out two more northern expeditions in 1819. One, under the command of William Parry, was to attempt to find the entrance to the Northwest Passage somewhere in Baffin Bay and navigate through it to the Pacific Ocean. The other expedition was to travel overland across North America to determine which seas the north-flowing rivers emptied into and map the coastlines. If possible, the two expeditions were to meet in the western Arctic.

While Franklin's early return to England in the autumn of 1818 frustrated him, his stay on home soil was brightened when he was chosen as one of the two expedition leaders for another attempt at finding a Northwest Passage. This time, however, instead of going by sea through the dangerous ice, the now 33-year-old naval officer would lead a small team on the long and arduous overland journey: Royal Navy surgeon Dr. John Richardson, age 31; John Hepburn, a 28-year-old Orkney sailor; and two Admiralty midshipmen, George Back, 22, and Robert Hood, the youngest at 21. Midshipman Back had served with Franklin on HMS *Trent* on the previous year's Arctic expedition.

Franklin's orders were to sail to the Hudson's Bay Company's (HBC) York Factory depot on the southwest shore of Hudson Bay. From there, he and his party were to travel by whatever means were available into the interior, in a northwesterly direction toward the Arctic coast. That meant going up the Hayes River to Norway House and beyond to Cumberland House—both HBC trading forts. They would then make their way across the Barrens to the northern coast of North America in the vicinity of the Coppermine River mouth and record the coast's latitude. Furthermore, Franklin was to explore as far east along the coast as possible and survey the land. If the expedition was successful, Franklin and his party would gather invaluable knowledge to add to existing navigational charts. Unfortunately, while the route might have looked feasible on paper, actually getting across such inhospitable terrain to the Arctic shores was to prove a challenging, exhausting and dangerous journey.

It must be said that Franklin was a rather odd choice for the overland expedition. He was brave—he had proved that many times—but he was overweight and knew nothing of river travel or of living off the land. Apart from his enforced sojourn on Australia's Wreck Reef as a young man, he had never camped out in the wilderness or been known to walk far. He liked to have three meals a day, served properly on china and with silver cutlery, and to take tea whenever he wanted it, which was often. Knowing his own shortcomings, Franklin must have wondered about his ability to take part in this expedition, let alone lead it. No doubt his drive for success in Arctic exploration had much to do with his decision to accept the position.

Not long before Franklin left London to join his ship, he went to visit Sir Alexander Mackenzie. Of that meeting Franklin wrote, "He afforded me, in the most open and kind manner, much valuable information and advice." At that time, Mackenzie was the recognized British expert on overland travel across the vast northern spaces of North America.

On Sunday, May 23, 1819, the five naval men boarded the HBC's three-masted, full-rigged ship *Prince of Wales* at Gravesend, on the south bank of the Thames River estuary. They sailed that night in company with two other HBC vessels—*Wear* and *Eddystone*—bound for a stop in the Orkney Islands and then across the North Atlantic to Hudson Bay.

After a slow but uneventful Atlantic crossing, the three ships entered Davis Strait, between Greenland and Labrador, on July 25 and met the first ice. For the next two weeks, the ships battled ice and fog until they sighted an indistinct Resolution Island at the entrance to Hudson Strait.

While trying to avoid heavy, drifting floes, *Prince of Wales* ran up onto rocks and sustained damage to her rudder, leaving her at the mercy of the winds and currents. A second grounding soon restored the rudder to its correct position, and the ship was under control again. The worst was yet to come. *Prince of Wales* was driven up against an iceberg and received more damage, causing her to take on water fast. In his account of the expedition, Franklin wrote of the scene, "After the first concussion the ship was driven along the steep and rugged side of this iceberg with such amazing rapidity that the destruction of the masts seemed inevitable."

Midshipman Hood described the collision with equal aplomb, "The projections of [the iceberg] threatened the masts, and tore away part of the chains. The iceberg was aground, and we were swept past it, with appalling noise, but with less real danger than we had already incurred."

All available hands, including Franklin and his men, worked the pumps and formed bucket brigades to keep the ship from sinking until the carpenters could make repairs. *Wear* and *Eddystone* had fared only marginally better. *Eddystone* had to put three boats out to tow her away from rocks. Of *Wear* there was no sign. Only later did Franklin and company learn what happened to her.

Strong tides, ice and more fog slowed progress through Hudson Strait so that the ships did not enter the northern extremity of Hudson Bay until August 19. En route, Franklin had his first encounter with the indigenous people. He wrote, "The ship was steered as near to the shore as the wind would permit, to give the Esquimaux inhabitants an opportunity of coming off to barter."

As the two ships ghosted toward the mouth of the Hayes River, those on board could see another ship at anchor in Five Fathom Hole, the anchorage for York Factory. *Prince of Wales* and *Eddystone* dropped their anchors within hailing distance on August 30. Their voyage from Gravesend had taken an unprecedented three months and one week. The ship waiting for them was the missing *Wear*. She too had been forced up on rocks off Resolution Island but had managed to claw herself off. Damaged but still afloat, and unable to see the other ships in the convoy, she had continued to Hudson Bay alone. The crews of the three ships were delighted to be in close company again.

York Factory stands on the north bank of the Hayes River, a short distance inland from Hudson Bay. In 1819, it was home to a small population of men, plus a few women and children. Outside the compound, or stockade, an ever-changing number of Swampy Cree families lived in moose hide teepees.

The main building at York Factory. Franklin and his expedition team started the 1819 overland journey to the Arctic from here.
ANTHONY DALTON

Franklin spent the next few days asking questions about the inland journey. The consensus was that his expedition should advance up the Hayes River to Norway House, nearly 400 miles (645 kilometres) away, then make its way via the north end of Lake Winnipeg and Cedar Lake to the HBC post at Cumberland House on the Saskatchewan River. From there, the recommended route was by way of the chain of HBC posts all the way to Great Slave Lake. Once at the big lake, the expedition party would strike out for the Arctic coast.

As soon as the upriver boat was ready to leave, Franklin and his party said their goodbyes and settled onto the mounds of baggage already aboard the York boat. The complement consisted of Franklin and his three officers, plus seaman John Hepburn, four Orkneymen and Charles Wilkes, a steersman from York Factory. The date was September 9, 1819. Ahead of them was a difficult passage across the Hudson Bay lowlands to the beginning of the rapids, 120 miles (193 kilometres) away. With a favourable wind, they stepped the mast and employed the rectangular sail to carry them upstream for the first day. After that, fighting against a strong current, they frequently had to drag the boats to make headway.

On September 17, they reached the first of the 47 cascades, where an HBC post known as The Rock stood, and found an easy portage route past the danger. From that point on, the boats climbed daily; the tripmen who had rowed the boats from York Factory unloaded them at the foot of each cascade and carried the cargo across portage routes to the next level stretch of river. They then returned and dragged the boats up the rapids using long ropes. At the more dangerous rapids they carried or dragged the boats across the portages as well.

At White Falls (now usually known as Robinson Falls), Franklin's dignity suffered when he fell into the river. Midshipman Robert Hood described the incident: "Mr. Franklin was traversing the banks, between two of the falls, when he slipped from the edge of a rock and rolled down a declivity 15 or 20 yards into the water. The current was not rapid, but the bank for a great extent continued too steep and slippery to afford him a firm grasp, and he was tantalized by sometimes touching the bottom, while he was, in spite of all his efforts, slowly approaching a [water] fall."

Franklin was lucky. From the top of the falls to the bottom there is an overall drop of well over 50 feet (15 metres). The final fall is almost one-third of that. By the time his companions reached his position and pulled him to safety on land, he was exhausted. Had he continued over the final drop of the falls, it is unlikely that he would have survived. It is to his credit, and due to his physical strength, that he soon recovered from his dunking, even though he also was suffering from whooping cough at the time.

Following traditional Cree hunting routes, the party arrived at Cumberland House on October 23. To get there, they had navigated over more than 50 rapids and through many miles of reed beds for a distance of 685 miles (1,100 kilometres) in 44 days—a respectable daily average of just over 15 miles (25 kilometres). Word had not reached Cumberland House of their impending arrival, causing some initial difficulty in housing the party. In fact, Franklin's crew had to help build extra accommodation for all the newcomers to share. With winter approaching and ice already forming on lakes and rivers, it was impossible to travel on the Barrens. Franklin had to remain at the post for many weeks, waiting for the waters and the ground to freeze. He did not set off again until mid-January 1820, and then without the full party.

A traditional York boat of the type that Franklin and his men would have used to ascend the Hayes River in 1819. ANTHONY DALTON

Franklin and Midshipman Back, with John Hepburn and four other men, left with four dogsleds heading northwest for Carlton House, Fort Edmonton and Fort Chipewyan. The snow was deep and the air temperature far below zero. For much of the way, all members of the group travelled on snowshoes, except for the two dog-team drivers. Following frozen rivers and lakes, it took them nine weeks to cover the 857 miles (1,380 kilometres) to Fort Chipewyan, on the western shores of Lake Athabasca.

Planning to use rivers as much as possible for the final long push to the Arctic shores when summer returned, Franklin had a large birchbark canoe built near Fort

Chipewyan. The canoe measured 32 feet 6 inches (11 metres 12 centimetres) in length and was 4 feet 10 inches (1 metre 47 centimetres) at its widest. Fragile though its construction certainly was, the canoe could handle up to 3,300 pounds (1,500 kilograms) of weight, made up of men and freight. The canoe itself weighed a mere 300 pounds (136 kilograms) and could be carried by two men across portages when empty.

Dr. Richardson and Robert Hood rejoined Franklin on July 13, arriving with two canoes and 10 men. Unfortunately, they came with only one day's provisions, which proved a huge disappointment to Franklin. He then had to scramble to collect enough food to get the expedition moving again. On July 18, the three canoes left Fort Chipewyan to travel down the Slave River to Great Slave Lake. On board were Franklin and his three officers, plus John Hepburn, 16 Canadians and a Chipewyan woman. The Slave River is notorious for its deadly rapids. Fortunately for Franklin, he had received concise information from traders at Fort Chipewyan and so knew what dangers to look for. In consequence, the three canoes descended the river without grave incident, although two of the canoes were damaged en route and needed serious repairs. The men also shot a bison to add to their larder.

Once off the river, they crossed Great Slave Lake to the north shore and the haven of Fort Providence, which was then situated just across the Yellowknife River from today's city of Yellowknife. Their route from Providence would take them up the Yellowknife River and overland to a series of narrow lakes, then down the Coppermine River to the sea. Before they could embark on this stage of the journey, they had to make friends with the chief of the local Copper people, some of whom would go with them as guides.

When they left Fort Providence on the afternoon of August 2, the expedition party had increased to 28, plus the wives of three of the Canadians. Three of the men were interpreters and guides. Among the Canadians was an Iroquois voyageur named Michel Teroahauté. He would figure largely on the return journey.

This part of the expedition, which would become increasingly difficult, was enlivened by an entourage of 17 Native canoes. The extensive Native fleet stayed with them for a few days before turning for home. Difficult portages and a meagre diet of fish and occasional meat slowed the journey toward the Coppermine River. In the middle of August, still many miles short of the Coppermine and with signs of the coming winter all around, Franklin sent Back and Hood ahead in a small canoe to look at the route they would face. Meanwhile, he and the rest of his entourage began the task of building winter quarters for themselves and for their stores near a source of fresh water and surrounded by pine trees that formed a natural windbreak. The largest building was a log cabin with five rooms to house Franklin and his officers. The 16 men under their command shared a smaller cabin. These two rather primitive dwellings would become known as Fort Enterprise.

In September, Franklin, Richardson and Hepburn set off with a Native guide to walk to the Coppermine River, even though the two midshipmen had already gone ahead to see it. For Franklin, it was a necessary personal reconnaissance because, apart from helping to build Fort Enterprise, he had nothing else to do. The round trip of over 40 miles (64 kilometres) took them just six days. When they returned to the planned winter quarters, they found Back and Hood had arrived the previous day. Once the log buildings had been completed, everyone prepared for the long winter. Those months were spent in hunting for food, writing up journals and waiting for the opportunity to get underway again. According to Franklin, they were not bored or idle. He wrote of that enforced layover, "We never found the time to hang heavy on our hands."

Early in June 1821, the expedition began preparations to leave Fort Enterprise and continue to the north. By June 14, all was in readiness, and they moved away from their winter home in mid-morning. To reach the first body of water, the canoes had to be hauled overland, each one by four men and two dogs. Marten Lake was still frozen, so the expedition team used its smooth surface to glide across at speed. Franklin, loaded down with a heavy bundle on his shoulders, fell through the ice into water just under the freezing point. He was rescued and dried without serious injury.

Robert Hood suffered a similar mishap the same day, also without injury.

Heavily laden, it took them two weeks of hard travel to reach the Coppermine River. To Franklin's disappointment, the Native hunters had wasted a lot of ammunition on the way but brought in very little food. Consequently, supplies were low and the hard-working men felt the lack of sustenance. Getting on the river at least removed some of the physical effort for a while. A few days later, they were fortunate in finding a herd of muskox and replenished the larder.

Progress down the Coppermine River required skill in descending the many rapids and hard work in portaging across or round thick ice jams. Franklin showed foresight in having all guns and ammunition taken out of the canoes and carried past each rapid, in case of accident. Knowing that their means of hunting, and therefore their survival, were safe made up for the loss of time this involved.

Nine miles (14 kilometres) short of the coast, the expedition reached Bloody Falls, the site of a massacre in 1771. In that year, Samuel Hearne, a fur trader and explorer working for the HBC, came down the Coppermine River with a party of Chipewyans. At the falls, they met a group of Inuit, and the Chipewyans killed them all. The bones of the unfortunate northerners still rested beside the falls when Franklin passed through.

Franklin's expedition reached the sea on July 18. Their

first view of Coronation Gulf (named by Franklin) showed a wide channel of open water bordering the land, with the sea beyond covered in ice. A trial with nets across the mouth of the river showed an abundance of fish. Franklin referred to them as salmon, but they were almost certainly Arctic char. There were also many seals in sight. Catching them, however, was a skill none of Franklin's men possessed.

Franklin's navigation, which was correct, showed that Samuel Hearne had erred in his observations. Franklin wrote, "It will be perceived that the mouth of the river, given by our observations, differs widely from that assigned by Mr. Hearne; but the accuracy of his description, conjoined with Indian information, assured us that we were at the very part he visited."

At this point, Franklin sent some of his party back to their base at Fort Enterprise. With them he sent the officers' journals and his own reports for shipment to England. Aware of the possibility of lack of food for his team on the return journey, he also cautioned the returning party to be sure to lay in a large stock of meat for them. With that, the two groups parted. One party went south, while Franklin and 19 others turned east along the coast of the Arctic sea. A comment from Franklin's book on the expedition reduces the agonies of the journey to the Arctic coast to basic facts: "The travelling distance from Fort Enterprise to the north of the Copper-Mine River is about three hundred and thirty-four miles. The canoes and baggage were dragged over snow and ice for one hundred and seventeen miles of this distance."

Despite his lack of physical fitness at the beginning of the expedition, and his complete lack of experience in wilderness travel, the indomitable John Franklin had acquitted himself well and reached the Arctic coast at the Coppermine River as ordered.

4

The Spectre
of Cannibalism

TRAVELLING THE WILD RIVERS TO the north had proved challenging. Foraging for sufficient fresh food to feed the expedition had also proved difficult. The voyage along the coast would be no less demanding. Birchbark canoes were excellent craft for river journeys, but they were not built for travelling through ice.

From July 20 until August 18, the expedition worked its way along the coast. En route they battled high winds, local fog, ice and powerful thunderstorms. Due to the large size of the party—20 men—obtaining fresh food was a constant problem that dominated Franklin's personal record of the journey. On August 18, they reached a prominence on the Kent Peninsula that Franklin named Point Turnagain; they had now covered and charted 555 miles (893 kilometres) of coastline, including a full survey of Bathurst Inlet and Melville Sound—a detour that took them nine days. En route, Franklin honoured his friends and a handful of superiors by naming geographical features for them.

Franklin didn't know it, but he was close to solving the riddle of the Northwest Passage. At Point Turnagain, he was only a few hundred miles from the Gulf of Boothia, the gateway via Lancaster Sound and Davis Strait to the Atlantic. On that day also, his friend William Parry was in Repulse Bay aboard HMS *Fury*, only 539 miles (867 kilometres) to the east in the northwest corner of Hudson Bay. He too was looking for a route that might become the Northwest Passage. Like his brother officer exploring the coast to the west, he was disappointed when he failed. Franklin, however, had come to the correct conclusion that the coast to the west would reach the open sea. He also expressed his belief that there was indeed a sea route from Point Turnagain to Hudson Bay. He was right, but the truth of those observations would not be known until after his death.

For Franklin and his men, ill-equipped as they were, going on was not an option. The only way for them to survive the coming winter was to quit the coast and get back to Fort Enterprise as soon as possible. Even that was a tall order. The journey would become a race against time and weather.

The Coppermine River route was discarded due to the scarcity of sufficient game along its course. Instead,

Franklin chose a rather more direct route back to base at Fort Enterprise. They would cross a wide stretch of open water to reach Arctic Sound, at the western shore of Bathurst Inlet. From there they would ascend the Hood River until it became too shallow. After that, they had no choice but to cross the Barrens, using any waterways possible and travelling on land when they had to.

Early in the return journey, on the shores of Arctic Sound, they were fortunate in shooting a few skinny female deer. Those sad creatures gave them enough food to rebuild their strength for a few days, and full bellies gave them hope for the future. On the Hood River they became the first white men to visit Wilberforce Falls. Named by Franklin for a renowned British philanthropist, the two sets of falls have a combined drop of 160 feet (49 metres).

When they eventually left the Hood River, they were looking at a cross-country hike of 149 miles (240 kilometres) to reach a former camp. To reduce the burden each would have to carry, all stores unnecessary for survival— and that included books—were packed in boxes and cached, perhaps to be retrieved sometime in the future.

Now the weather turned worse. Heavy rains were followed by snow drifting in places to a depth of three feet (one metre). With only draughty canvas tents for shelter and old, well-worn blankets for bedding, everyone suffered from the extreme cold and consequent lack of sleep each night. To add to their misery, the food was almost gone and all were hungry. Franklin became so weak that he passed out and had to be revived with a small amount of soup. He wrote of the conditions as they set off once more:

> The ground was covered a foot deep with snow, the margins of the lakes were encrusted with ice, and the swamps over which we had to pass were entirely frozen; but the ice not being sufficiently strong to bear us, we frequently plunged knee-deep in water. Those who carried the canoes were repeatedly blown down by the violence of the wind, and they often fell, from making an insecure step on a slippery stone; on one of these occasions, the largest canoe was so much broken as to be rendered utterly unserviceable.

The loss of the large canoe was, as Franklin put it, "a serious disaster." However, as they had not eaten properly for three days, they put the wreckage to good use. Franklin wrote, "As the accident could not be remedied, we turned it to the best account, by making a fire of the bark and timbers . . . and cooked the remainder of our portable soup and arrowroot." It wasn't much of a meal for half-starved men, but it helped.

Because of the snow, the men marched in single file, one behind the other, each treading in footprints made by the leader. Robert Hood walked directly behind the first man, constantly checking compass bearings to keep them on the right track. They were fortunate in flushing out a flock of partridges and were able to bring down 10 of them. With a substantial supply of lichen (called *tripe de roche* by the Canadian voyageurs) scraped from rocks, they had the makings of a meal. A few slim willow branches dug out of the snow made a fire to cook the food.

Without the large canoe, wide river crossings became a regular trial. Most of them were fast-running and littered with rapids. Paddlers and passengers often overbalanced the small canoe in the turbulent waters; as a consequence, the men were soaked from at least the waist down, and this in temperatures varying between 17 and 24°F (-8 and -4°C).

On September 22, the remaining canoe was dropped and damaged beyond repair. Now the party was in real trouble. River crossings would prove dangerous, if not fatal. Lakes would be impassable. By this time, the voyageurs were convinced they were going to die, and Franklin found it impossible to control them. Some threw away their burdens; others scavenged food and failed to share it. With so little game available, they were all reduced to eating their old shoes, including the once-finicky John Franklin.

Approximately 40 miles (64 kilometres) from Fort Enterprise, they again found the upper reaches of the Coppermine River, which they had to cross. The width at this point, just above a series of rapids, was an estimated 130 yards (119 metres). The water temperature would have been only slightly above freezing point, and the river was fast. Falling in would prove fatal. First, they made an unsuccessful attempt to build a raft out of willows.

When that failed, one of the voyageurs fashioned a canoe from tent canvas covering a willow frame. It worked well enough for the party to cross one at a time; a rope pulled the canoe back across the river after each sortie. The date was October 4.

Franklin now sent Midshipman Back and three voyageurs to travel ahead to Fort Enterprise to enlist help from local Natives, if they could be found. Two of the voyageurs remaining with Franklin's party were too weak by this time to continue and fell by the wayside to die in the snow. At this point, from the advantage of hindsight, Franklin made a significant error of judgment. He allowed his fellow officers to talk him into further separating the party. As a result, Dr. Richardson, Robert Hood and John Hepburn volunteered to stay behind and wait for help. Hood was much too weak to have gone any farther anyway. Franklin invited any voyageurs who felt physically weak to stay with the officers. None did.

Franklin started out with serious misgivings about leaving his fellow officers, but he felt he had little choice. Starvation or death from cold were now real possibilities. The following day, two voyageurs, Belanger and Michel Teroahauté, complained of weakness and begged to be allowed to return to Richardson, Hood and Hepburn. When Franklin finally agreed to release them, Teroahauté asked about the direction and distance to Fort Enterprise—knowledge, perhaps, he felt he would need in the future.

Only a mile or so farther along the trail, Perrault, another voyageur, asked to be allowed to return with his two companions. Franklin agreed and Perrault turned back. Soon another, Fontano, refused to go on, and he too followed their tracks back to the camp. Franklin's group now comprised only five people, including himself.

Travelling as hard as they could, the small group reached Fort Enterprise without delay, only to find it deserted and devoid of food. There was a note from Midshipman Back. He had arrived two days earlier and had gone in search of Natives to help them. Franklin's disappointment was acute. He wrote, "It would be impossible to describe our sensations after entering this miserable abode, and discovering how we had been neglected: the whole party shed tears, not so much for our own fate, as for that of our friends in the rear, whose lives depended entirely on our sending immediate relief from this place."

Before long it became obvious that Franklin was the strongest of his small party, if not physically, then certainly mentally. He now took on the additional role of collecting *tripe de roche* for food and willows for a fire. Unknown to Franklin, it is almost certain that by this time Teroahauté had murdered Belanger and Perrault and eaten parts of their flesh. More horrors were to follow.

On October 29, Dr. Richardson and Hepburn arrived at Fort Enterprise to join Franklin and his men. Hood was not with the new arrivals. Richardson explained that

Hood was dead, and so was Michel Teroahauté. Belanger, Perrault and Fontano had never reached the camp. Only later, after an insignificant meal, did Richardson tell the full story.

Teroahauté had shot Robert Hood in the back of the head on October 20. It was obviously a deliberate act. Hepburn was close by at the time, and although he did not see the action, he did see Teroahauté behind Hood immediately after the shot. Teroahauté insisted that Hood had shot himself, either by accident or by design. Richardson and Hepburn were not convinced. The shot that killed Hood had entered the back of his skull and exited from the front. In fear for their lives, Hepburn volunteered to shoot Teroahauté. Richardson made his own decision. He wrote, "I determined, however, as I was thoroughly convinced of the necessity of such a dreadful act, to take the whole responsibility on myself; and immediately upon Michel's coming up, I put an end to his life by shooting him through the head with a pistol."

At the beginning of November, two more of the voyageurs died of starvation and exposure—perhaps also of despair. A few days later, on November 7, relief arrived. Three Natives sent by Back had enough food with them to revive the three emaciated Englishmen and the last of the voyageurs. They also brought word that Back and his companions were now strong enough to continue on to Fort Providence and would meet them there eventually.

"Captain Franklin, R.N.," a portrait painted soon after the 1819–22 overland expedition.

PETER WINKWORTH COLLECTION. LIBRARY AND ARCHIVES CANADA R9266-3036

Franklin, Richardson, Hepburn and their two remaining voyageurs left Fort Enterprise with the Natives on December 1. Ahead of them lay more wilderness terrain, but this time they had skilled help and regular food. Three days later, two Canadian voyageurs coming up from Fort Providence met them on the trail. They had letters for them and a change of clothes. Among the letters was the news from England that Franklin had been promoted to captain and the two midshipmen to lieutenants. Hood, of course, would never know of his promotion. On arriving at Fort Providence, the long ordeal was over. There they were reunited with George Back and spent the rest of the winter at the fort, slowly regaining strength for the long journey back to York Factory by way of Fort Chipewyan and Cumberland House.

Franklin's depleted party left Fort Providence on May 26 and arrived back at York Factory on July 14, 1822. He calculated that they had travelled 5,550 miles (8,932 kilometres) since they left the HBC post in 1819, all of that distance on foot and in small boats. They still had to cross Hudson Bay and the North Atlantic to get home, but the hard travelling was finally over, for the moment.

5

Overland to the
Polar Sea, Again

AT LEAST TWO WOMEN FOCUSED their romantic attentions on John Franklin. First was the lovely and intelligent Eleanor Anne Porden. She was frail, though quite vivacious. The daughter of a celebrated architect, Eleanor was an accomplished poet and interested enough in scientific subjects to be able to discuss them with confidence and knowledge. Franklin asked to meet her after he read some verses she had written about his Arctic expedition of 1818. According to Eleanor's friend Jane Griffin (who would later become Franklin's second wife), "An eye witness of their first interview ... saw at once how their acquaintance was likely to end."

John Franklin was a 32-year-old lieutenant in His Majesty's Navy when the two first met late in 1818. Eleanor was 23. After a five-year courtship, much of which was spent apart, Franklin married Eleanor on August 6, 1823. They had a daughter, also called Eleanor, the following year, but the happy marriage was doomed. In January 1825, Franklin's wife was discovered to be suffering from tuberculosis. At the time, Franklin, now elevated in rank to captain, was deep into plans for a return to the Arctic the following month. He had already selected his team and accumulated the materials he required. Despite Eleanor's serious illness, it was too late for him to back out or to delay the start. Besides, he was an officer in the Royal Navy. He had his duty to perform.

While he would travel overland, again with Dr. John Richardson at his side, his friend Sir William Parry would take a more northerly route by sea and attempt a passage down Prince Regent's Inlet. The two expeditions hoped to meet in the Arctic and once and for all prove the existence of the Northwest Passage. Franklin's orders were to descend the Mackenzie River to the Arctic Ocean and then continue west along the north shore of Alaska and follow the coastline southwest from Point Barrow to Icy Cape. There, if he had not already linked up with Parry, he was to meet Captain Beechey in HMS *Blossom*. Beechey had been sent on the long haul via the North and South Atlantic Oceans, round Cape Horn, north across the Pacific and through the Bering Strait to wait in Kotzebue Sound for news of Franklin's overland party.

Dr. Richardson's instructions were to leave Franklin at the mouth of the Mackenzie River and travel east to chart the coast until he reached the extent of Franklin's discoveries during the summer of 1821. This time, instead of relying on fragile birchbark canoes, Franklin would have the luxury of two purpose-built, lightweight wooden boats for the inland journey. Franklin designed the boats himself and their construction was supervised at Woolwich by Captain David Buchan, Franklin's commanding officer on the Arctic expedition of 1818. The largest of the two boats was only 26 feet (8 metres) long, yet said to be capable of carrying nine men plus three tons of supplies. The crew called it the *Lion*. A third canvas boat, designed for emergency use only, was collapsible. Due to its shape, it earned the name *Walnut Shell*.

The original plan had been that Franklin and Dr. Richardson would be accompanied by draughtsman/artist Lieutenant John Bushnan, Midshipman E.N. Kendall, plus a naturalist and a surveyor. In addition to the officers and scientists, there would be four marines, all considered to be good marksmen, and an unspecified number of common sailors. Unfortunately for Franklin, Bushnan died suddenly in the summer of 1824; against Franklin's wishes, Barrow replaced him with Lieutenant George Back. History does not tell us what the differences were between Franklin and Back, only that Franklin wrote to Richardson, "You know I could have no desire for his company but I do not see how I could decline it, if the Admiralty press the matter, without . . . publicly making an exposure of his incapacity in many respects." History has shown that Back was arrogant and opinionated throughout his naval career and showed little respect for other people's feelings. It's possible that these undesirable traits upset the rather gentle-minded Franklin.

Captain Franklin said goodbye to his ailing wife and healthy baby daughter and set sail from Liverpool on February 16, 1825, with his expedition team, bound for New York. From there, they followed rivers and lakes to the north and west, including a visit to Niagara Falls en route. At Penetanguishene, on the shores of Lake Huron, he learned of his wife's death. She had passed away while he was crossing the Atlantic, just six days after he left England. His young daughter had been sent to live with his sister. There was nothing he could do but continue the expedition.

Franklin crossed the continent diagonally to Lake Athabasca and then followed the Slave River to Great Slave Lake. From Fort Resolution, on the lake's southern shore, he continued down the Mackenzie River to the Great Bear River and up to Great Bear Lake. While George Back and a few men took care of arrangements for the team to spend the winter of 1825 at an abandoned fur-trading post on the shore of Great Bear Lake, the rest of the expedition split into two. Richardson and a few men explored the north shore of the lake. Franklin and a small entourage left the site on August 8 and travelled down the Mackenzie River to the Beaufort Sea. After a brief look at the salt water and its attendant ice, Franklin returned to the selected winter quarters, now named Fort Franklin, where he arrived on September 5.

By this time the expedition numbered 50 people. They were "Peter Warren Dease, Chief Trader of HBC, five [Royal Navy] officers, nineteen British seamen and marines, nine Canadians, and two Eskimos . . . together with Chipewyan hunters, three women, six children, and one Indian lad." All these people had to be fed. Inevitably, rations began to run low. By February 1826, the meat stocks had been used and each person was limited to four small herrings per day. The storeroom still held a substantial supply of pemmican, but Franklin preferred to keep this for summer travel or for a · real emergency.

The winter, as expected, was severe, but the officers and men found hunting and reading helped pass the dark months. Spring, according to Franklin's journal, arrived on May 24, 1826. He wrote, "The mosquitoes appeared, feeble at first, but, after a few days, they became vigorous and tormenting. The first flower, a tussilago [possibly *Tussilago farfara*], was gathered on the 27th. Before the close of the month, several others were in bloom, of which the most abundant was the white anemone."

As the weather improved, the game returned and the slight risk of famine was averted. Caribou and the first

ducks and swans of the season soon filled empty bellies and
a sense of well-being came over the settlement. At the end
of the third week in June, the rivers and lakes were start-
ing to open up as the winter ice melted. The only drawback
to the good weather was that it meant the winter quarters
were invaded by "Dog-Ribs [Indians] who now visited us
in great numbers, without bringing any supplies." The visitors hung around for a couple of weeks before moving on to
their summer fishing grounds.

In addition to the two boats Franklin had hauled from
England, the carpenters had built a third, slightly larger,
seagoing boat, which they named *Reliance*. All three boats
were equipped with oars and sails. The exploring parties
would number 28 men, divided among the three boats.
Franklin wrote out strict orders for his leaders and for HBC
trader Dease, who would look after Fort Franklin in their
absence. Aware of the need for specifics, as the possibilities for radical deviations from the plans were enormous,
he instructed Dease to maintain the fort and keep it supplied with food until the spring of 1828. Although Franklin
hoped to cover the coast from the Mackenzie River delta to
the Chukchi Sea and meet up with HMS *Blossom*, in which
case he and his team would continue on the navy ship to
Canton, China, he knew only too well the obstacles in his
path. Dease had to keep Fort Franklin open long enough for
the expedition to return to if necessary.

The three boats and 28 men left Fort Franklin on June 22

and set off down the short length of the Great Bear River to the Mackenzie, then turned northwest on that great river toward the sea. On July 4, Richardson's party left Franklin and took an eastern channel through the Mackenzie delta to begin their coastal survey. Franklin, in *Lion*, and George Back, in the newly built *Reliance*, followed a western channel to the Beaufort Sea. The two boats reached the river's mouth on July 7, and Franklin's party immediately ran into problems with local Natives. Unaware of the white man's ideas regarding possessions, the Natives stole everything they could get their hands on, even slashing at the officers' coats with their knives to collect the shiny buttons. For over 24 hours, mayhem reigned as the Natives stole and the beleaguered explorers struggled to recover their belongings without resorting to the use of firearms, although many blows were exchanged.

By the time the boats continued west on July 9, Franklin's men were frustrated and angry. They later learned that many of the Natives had argued to kill all the white men and take everything. Getting back on the water was the best cure for sailors. Ice, however, soon blocked the route, and they had to retreat some distance to find a suitable campsite. Again they came to the attention of a large group of Natives and again they had to work hard to protect their belongings.

On the move again, they landed on Herschel Island, so named by Franklin, which would become an important whaling station later in the 19th century. Thick fog and impossible ice conditions slowed the journey west. Franklin described the ongoing problems in detail:

> We were stopped by the ice which adhered to the reef, and was unbroken to seaward. Imagining we saw water at some distance beyond this barrier, we were induced to drag the boats across the reef, and launch them into the channel on the inside, in the hope of reaching it. This proved to be a bay, at the head of which we arrived in a short time. It was then discovered that a fog hanging over the ice had been mistaken for water.

That unfortunate event caused them to retreat a few miles and search for open water. At Prudhoe Bay, after suffering similar daily difficulties in their passage along the coast, they were stopped by a gale. Now it fell to Franklin, the expedition's leader, to decide whether to go on and hope to meet up with HMS *Blossom* or to retrace their route to Fort Franklin.

If HMS *Blossom* had not reached Icy Cape, Franklin knew that his men could be in extreme danger. They would be in unknown territory and too far from Fort Franklin for a retreat when bad weather began, as it would in a few weeks. Because the weather was already against them, Franklin elected to return to the fort via the Mackenzie River. His rationale for this decision made perfect sense:

[This journey] shows the difficulties of navigating such a coast, even during the finest part of the summer; if, indeed, any portion of a season which had been marked by a constant succession of fogs and gales could be called fine. No opportunity of advancing had been let slip, after the time of our arrival in the Arctic Sea; and the unwearied zeal and exertion of the crews had been required, for an entire month, to explore the ten degrees of longitude between Herschel Island and our present situation, I had, therefore, no reason to suppose that the ten remaining degrees could be navigated in much less time.

Despite his decision, Franklin was not happy about turning back. His journal shows a certain bitterness, tempered by the need to look after his men:

It was with no ordinary pain that I could now bring myself even to think of relinquishing the great object of my ambition, and of disappointing the flattering confidence that had been reposed in my exertions. But I had higher duties to perform than the gratification of my own feelings; and a mature consideration of all the above matters forced me to the conclusion, that we had reached that point beyond which perseverance would be rashness, and our best efforts must be fruitless.

Before leaving the Prudhoe Bay area on August 21, the group built a square cairn from a pile of driftwood and flew a red flag from its apex. Under the timber, they buried a letter for Captain Parry and some tokens of identification, such as a silver medal and some British coins.

Franklin, of course, could not have known, but *Blossom* was in the vicinity of Icy Cape at the time, and a party of her men were no more than 160 miles (257 kilometres) from Franklin's position when he turned for home. Parry was far away to the east, trying to find a route through the passage. Franklin and his men arrived back at Fort Franklin on September 21. The Franklin and Parry expeditions had not met in the Arctic, but another section of the elusive passage had been explored.

Determined not to suffer the deprivations of his previous overland expedition, Franklin had made sure that sufficient food was available for all members of his party at every stop along the way. More was cached at appropriate locations in case conditions necessitated a retreat.

Meanwhile, Dr. John Richardson had taken his party east along the coast from the Mackenzie River delta and reached the mouth of the Coppermine River without incident. Combined with Franklin's westerly explorations, Richardson's side journey had filled in even more blanks on Arctic maps. Apart from adding information to maps of the Arctic coastline, including a survey of the western channel of the Mackenzie River delta, the two-pronged expedition achieved little else of value; even so, Franklin's reports would be well-received in London. By the end of the first week of September, all members of the expedition were safely "home" at the winter quarters, now known as Fort Franklin. Musing on the Northwest Passage, Franklin wrote in his notes on the expedition: "We traced the coast, westward from the mouth of the Mackenzie, three hundred and seventy-four miles, without having found one harbour in which a ship could find shelter."

As it was far too late in the season to start on the long journey across the continent to find a ship to take them home, the expedition members settled in for the winter. At roughly four degrees south of the Arctic Circle, Fort Franklin would have been a cold and dark abode for the dreary months until the sun returned, but the expedition members were hard men, used to fending for themselves, and survived without incident.

When the snow began to clear in the spring, they shook off the torpidity of winter and began the trek on rivers and muskeg halfway across a continent to Norway House, at the northern extremity of Lake Winnipeg. From there, instead of taking the Hayes River route to York Factory, Franklin and some of his men followed successive waterways to Montreal, where he arrived on August 18. By September 26, 1827, they were stepping ashore on home soil in Liverpool. They had been away for two years, seven months and two weeks.

CHAPTER

6

A *Rainbow*
in the Mediterranean

NOT LONG AFTER RETURNING FROM the Arctic, Franklin, a 41-year-old widower, began to show interest in his late wife's friend, the forceful Jane Griffin. He visited her parents' home and left his calling card. Jane, a healthy, free-thinking, independent lady of 36, was at that time travelling somewhere in Europe. When she returned, they met at her home and occasionally attended society functions together. The couple soon announced their engagement and planned a November 1828 wedding in England.

Prior to the wedding, in the summer of 1828, Franklin and the Griffin family travelled to Russia. Franklin travelled separately from the family and met up with them in St. Petersburg. Having explored and mapped the north coast of Alaska as far as Prudhoe Bay, which was then Russian territory, Franklin was entertained in Russia in high style. Jane, as his fiancée, was usually at his side. From Russia, they all travelled home together in September by way of Germany and the Netherlands, with stops in Hamburg, Amsterdam and Leyden. They were married at Stanmore on November 5 and spent a short honeymoon in Paris. There, in addition to meeting the future king of France, Franklin had the pleasure of greeting the former Duchess of Angoulême, now Madame la Dauphine, whom he had escorted home to France when he was second in command of HMS *Forth*.

As a result of his Arctic endeavours, both successes and failures, Franklin was knighted by King George IV in April 1829 and received an honorary degree in civil law from Oxford University the same year. His friend, William Parry, was similarly honoured at the same event in Oxford's Sheldonian Theatre. But despite his rewards, Captain Franklin's career was going nowhere. The Royal Navy had called a halt to northern exploration, and with no wars to fight, there was little for naval officers to do. He was offered a reasonably lucrative business appointment in Australia but turned it down, still hoping for command of a new Arctic expedition.

Although the Admiralty had halted northern explora-tion, there was an Arctic expedition in the planning stages, and as it had been sanctioned by the Admiralty prior to the embargo, it showed every chance of going ahead.

Unfortunately for Franklin, he was not invited to join the endeavour. Leadership was given to John Ross, and his nephew, James Clark Ross, was to be second-in-command. When the expedition ship, a converted and strengthened paddle steamer, was fitting out at Woolwich, Sir John Franklin and Jane went on board to look at her in May 1829. Named *Victory*, the steamer was hardly suited to an Atlantic crossing, far less an Arctic expedition. Even so, Franklin must have watched the departure with envious eyes. He was still an unemployed naval officer on half pay. He could put up with the half pay but disliked being idle.

Franklin spent more than another year at leisure in England. His sedentary life caused him to put on weight even as he yearned for action. At the end of August 1830, his prayers were answered. He was recalled by the navy and given command of HMS *Rainbow*, a 26-gun frigate. The man who had become something of an expert on the Arctic, and who had been lobbying to return to the North, was then sent in the opposite direction—to the sunny and warm Mediterranean. *Rainbow* set sail from Portsmouth on September 11, bound for Malta.

Jane and young Eleanor remained in England for a year, while Franklin and *Rainbow* patrolled the Mediterranean, showing the flag and defending British interests. When Jane joined her husband in 1831, Eleanor stayed put with relatives in England. Jane travelled to Malta, with a stop in Cadiz, Spain, en route. With her went her father, her maid and another

Lady Jane Franklin, the explorer's second wife, would prove to be his most stalwart supporter.
AUSTRALIAN GOVERNMENT DEPARTMENT OF THE ENVIRONMENT AND WATER RESOURCES

attendant. Old Mr. Griffin found the journey too much to handle and soon returned to his English home, while Jane and her depleted entourage continued to Malta, where her husband waited. Due to a quarantine on all arrivals, a holdover from the dreadful plague of 1813, John and Jane were unable to meet, except at a distance, for the first 48 hours.

For the next two years, Jane wandered the lands surrounding the Mediterranean, studying their cultures and visiting historical sites while her husband was patrolling the large, almost landlocked sea. They met whenever possible, sometimes for a few weeks, sometimes a few months. Often they missed each other by no more than a couple of days.

In the spring of 1832, *Rainbow* was deployed to Greece to settle a series of petty business disputes between local merchants, who claimed to be British, and the governor of Patras. That was followed by a show of force to protect Patras from a minor revolt. Apart from those events, life in the Mediterranean arena was peaceful and relatively comfortable for officers and, to some extent, for common sailors as well.

Franklin and his wife lived for a time in rented accommodation on Corfu, until she went travelling. In April 1833, they were both in Malta. With his ship in the naval dockyard at Valletta, Franklin and his wife enjoyed a few weeks together in a hotel. Most of the time, *Rainbow*, with her captain aboard, patrolled the Mediterranean east of Malta, calling at ports wherever Franklin was ordered.

While Franklin cruised in the sun, his Royal Navy contemporaries, the two Rosses, were trudging about in the Arctic in the less than serviceable *Victory*. It must have been particularly galling for Franklin, as he had recommended the navy send him to those same icy areas as far back as

1828. Despite his frustration, there was nothing he could do about his ambitions while on duty at Malta. Only in England, within calling distance of the Admiralty and persons of influence, could he achieve his personal goals.

After a little more than three years based at Malta and solving petty disputes in the eastern Mediterranean, toward the end of 1833, Franklin and *Rainbow* received orders to return to England. Jane, still travelling the exotic lands of the Near East and at that time in Alexandria, Egypt, did not get home until the following October. For Franklin, the return to England gave him the opportunity to continue lobbying for a return to the Arctic. Once again, he would be disappointed.

7

Governor of Van Diemen's Land

DESPITE HIS EXPRESSED WISH TO be given command of further Arctic endeavours, in 1836 Sir John Franklin was again passed by and left on shore in England, trying to hide his frustration. His despair can only be imagined when his former subordinate, now his equal in rank, Captain George Back, was given command of the navy ship HMS *Terror* and sent on an expedition to attempt to chart the coastline between Prince Regent Inlet and Point Turnagain. Back was ordered to attempt to make his approach through Wager Bay or Repulse Bay, both in the northwest corner of Hudson Bay. Once again, Franklin's knowledge of the North and his experience accumulated on three expeditions on land and sea, covering many thousands of miles, was set aside.

Back's expedition would prove to be a failure, offering little new information for cartographers or the Admiralty, except for the knowledge that both bays were just that and not navigable routes to the west. HMS *Terror* suffered severe damage from ice in Hudson Bay and staggered back to England in late 1837, with all hands safe and well. Although the expedition had not achieved any of its objectives, Back went on to receive a knighthood for his efforts.

Meanwhile, with no captaincy of a Royal Navy ship on offer and no Arctic expedition available, Franklin needed something to occupy his mind and absorb his energies. He was eventually offered the governorship of Antigua. On advice from others, and especially from Jane, he declined the post. Then he received another offer. Once again, instead of the North, he was asked to go south, but not to a polar region. This time, he accepted; he could do little else. Although the posting was about as far away from England as he could possibly get, an associate at the Admiralty assured Franklin that should a naval ship become available, there was still a possibility that he would get another command. It was, at best, a forlorn hope.

Franklin's new position would be governor of Van Diemen's Land (now Tasmania). Barrow, now Sir John, sent his congratulations. In August 1836, Franklin and Jane set off for Australia with a considerable entourage: 12-year-old Eleanor; two maids; two nieces, Sophia Cracroft and Mary Franklin; Franklin's aide-de-camp, Alexander Elliot; surveyor, old friend and shipmate John Hepburn; and the Maconochie family. Captain Alexander Maconochie had been recommended to Franklin as a private secretary. Accepting him was to prove a huge mistake. Maconochie's family included his wife and six unruly children.

At that time, Van Diemen's Land was home to a penal colony at Port Arthur, a few miles from Hobart Town, with a population of an estimated 18,000 convicts. In addition, the heart-shaped island was home to another 24,000 whites, many of whom were former convicts. The indigenous Aboriginal population had been so decimated by three generations of white incursion and attacks that fewer than 100 were left by the time the Franklins arrived.

The penal colony was a dreadful place in a beautiful setting. Men, women and children, convicts all, lived in a compound with high, grey stone walls on the green Tasman peninsula. Many of them had been jailed for extremely petty crimes, such as stealing a few onions. There were three separate prisons in the area: one for men, one for women and, perhaps the cruellest of all, one for children.

Franklin's predecessor as governor of Van Diemen's Land was Colonel George Arthur, a self-serving and unpopular official who had lined his own pockets with as much money as he could during his tenure and earned the mistrust and extreme dislike of his subjects in the process. Franklin was a different governor altogether; he was a religious man and an honest man—the antithesis of George Arthur. The

The remains of the penal colony at Port Arthur on the Tasman Peninsula. ANTHONY DALTON

free residents of Van Diemen's Land looked to their new governor to correct the wrongs perpetrated by his predecessor and to improve their lives, but it didn't happen. At that time, Sir John was too gentle and too busy trying to please everyone to take a hard line. He saw good in most people, while often failing to look behind the façade. Lady Franklin was perhaps more astute and quicker to judge people, but she was the governor's wife, not the governor.

Franklin got off to a bad start by publicly complimenting the recently departed governor and his accomplishments. To add to his problems, two of Colonel Arthur's nephews by marriage were in positions of power in Hobart Town, one was colonial secretary and the other was the chief police magistrate. Franklin saw no reason to replace them with his own men, so kept them on the payroll. It was another strike against him as far as the citizens were concerned.

Maconochie had hoped to be given the post of colonial secretary. When it became clear that the post was unavailable he also turned against Franklin and began to agitate behind his back. Captain Montagu, the colonial secretary, rather liked Franklin—at first. Montagu wrote, "He is in very bad hands and his Private Secretary [Maconochie], who is a very different person, will ruin him in twelve months and make his government a bed of thorns."

Maconochie managed to create problems in much less than one year. It only took him three months to undermine Franklin's position as governor. The outspoken Maconochie is said to have told Lady Franklin that he was aiming for "not only the highest offices of the Executive under the Governor, but for the Governorship itself." Even the kindly Franklin could not ignore the hostility, and Maconochie was fired. Yet, despite the uncomfortable situation, Maconochie and his family continued to reside at Government House with the Franklins for some time.

Maconochie and his family stayed in Hobart Town until he was recalled to England in 1844. Throughout his sojourn in Van Diemen's Land, he created dissent and diplomatic difficulties for Governor Franklin. Beyond the Maconochie affair, public infighting between other members of the governor's senior staff added to his worries.

At times, although she certainly championed her husband, Lady Franklin could create her own tensions. Tasmania is home to three species of venomous snakes. One of Jane's more bizarre projects was to attempt to eradicate the reptiles from Tasmania. Because a bounty was paid for each snake's head handed in, the project proved popular with locals, and with the convicts, although it provoked much amusement at Jane's expense in higher circles. When she lowered the offered bounty by 75 percent, her popularity went down with it. Long believed to be the motivating force behind Sir John, she must have been upset to read a few sarcastic lines about herself in the *Colonial Times*: "Can anyone for a moment believe that she and her clique do not reign paramount here?"

On August 15, 1840, the Franklins received a visit from a Royal Navy surveying expedition to Antarctica, which hoped to reach the south magnetic pole. Commanded by Captain James Clark Ross with Captain Francis Crozier as his second, the expedition featured two ships, HMS *Erebus* and HMS *Terror*, both of which would feature largely in Franklin's future. Lady Jane Franklin insisted the senior officers stay with the Franklins at Government House in Hobart Town during their layover en route to the south. John Franklin, of course, was delighted to have such special company.

The two ships remained in the Hobart Town area for over two months. During those weeks, expedition members established a magnetic observatory overlooking the town. Most of the hard physical construction work was done by a couple of hundred convicts. The ships left in November 1840, and by April 1841, the expedition was back in Hobart Town, having failed to reach the elusive goal of the south magnetic pole due to ice conditions. Instead, they had taken magnetic observations on a series of islands and charted previously unknown sections of Antarctica. They had also named bights, sounds and mountains, including two named after their ships: Mount Erebus and Mount Terror.

Planning to return to Antarctica in the spring, Ross and Crozier spent the next few months working at their observatory, often assisted by the enthusiastic Governor Franklin. They also threw a society ball on the decks of their ships, which was much enjoyed by Hobart Town's hoi polloi.

There was a hint of romance in the air that Tasmanian autumn. Franklin's niece, Sophia Cracroft, took a shine to James Clark Ross, even though he was known to have a fiancée in England. Crozier, an Irishman (therefore not considered a gentleman) and a bachelor, fell hard for Sophia, but she ignored his obvious attentions. With Crozier saddened by Miss Cracroft's lack of interest in him, the expedition ships departed for mainland Australia, New Zealand and again to Antarctica in July.

For the next two years, the diplomatic feuds continued at Government House and in Hobart Town, leaving most of the unpleasantness heaped on Sir John's shoulders. Franklin and Montagu had fallen out in the autumn of 1841. After that Montagu was said to have adopted a policy of obstruction in his dealings with the governor. Tired of Montagu's disloyal attitude, Franklin suspended him in January 1842. Montagu returned to England a month later, vowing hatred for Franklin. Montagu's revenge was not long in coming.

Lord Stanley, the British colonial secretary, who was not one of Franklin's admirers, offered his official judgement on Montagu's suspension. In a long dispatch to Franklin in September 1842, he showed himself to be entrenched on Montagu's side. One paragraph in particular condemns Franklin: "Reluctant as I am to employ a single expression which is likely to be unwelcome to you, I am compelled to add that your proceedings in this case of Mr. Montagu do not appear to me to have been well judged, and that your suspension of him from office is not, in my opinion, sufficiently vindicated."

Unfortunately for Franklin, the gist of the dispatch was relayed to other sources in Hobart Town, possibly by Montagu himself, who had read the contents only days after Stanley wrote it. The unpleasant parts of the dispatch, those condemning Franklin, were soon spread among the populace by local newspapers and gossip before Franklin had received the full document. Flushed with indignation, Sir John threatened to resign if the British government could not show more confidence in his decisions. It was too little, too late. Although Franklin could not have known it, the decision to replace him had already been made, but the official letter of recall would take six months to reach him. Until that time, he had to stiffen his back, hold his head high and do his best to ignore the often slanderous newspaper reports on his administration.

Finally, suffering under a cloud of political intrigue, Franklin took his extended family home to England at the end of his six-year tenure in 1843. He was sad and disillusioned. The only cure for his ills would be to obtain a command and go back to sea or on another expedition.

8

To the Northwest Passage

AFTER HIS INVOLVEMENT YEARS BEFORE in three northern expeditions, the Arctic lands had captivated Franklin almost to the point of obsession. When a new expedition was being considered in 1844, Franklin and his lady went into high gear, writing to and talking with anyone who could influence the decision-making process. Acknowledged experts such as James Clark Ross, William Parry and James Fitzjames, among others, were being considered as possible leaders. In fact, the highly experienced polar explorer James Clark Ross was Sir John Barrow's first choice to lead the expedition. He declined the opportunity, wanting to spend more time at home with his wife and family. Parry had retired. So, the die appeared to fall at the feet of James Fitzjames.

Franklin was in the running, but against his passion, knowledge and experience, as far as the authorities were concerned, was his age. By 1845 he was 59, almost 60, and he was overweight. To add to those obvious drawbacks, he had not been to the Arctic for close to 20 years. However, Franklin was well-known to the decision makers and the general public as a fine seaman and explorer and he was popular enough in the right circles. Fitzjames was 26 years his junior and a virtual unknown, although he had polar experience, most recently with Ross in Antarctica, and he was considered to be the handsomest man in the Royal Navy. With Ross and Parry out of the running, Franklin won the toss and got the job.

Finding the Northwest Passage had been Sir John Barrow's passion for three decades. He was now 80 years old and close to retirement. All that stood between success or failure was about 200 miles (320 kilometres) of uncharted waters between Barrow Strait, at the western end of Lancaster Sound, and the open water on the south side of King William Land (now known to be an island) that had been seen by Dease and Simpson's HBC expedition of 1838–39. In his proposal to the Admiralty, Barrow substantiated his belief in the existence of the passage and its importance to Britain, writing, "If the completion of the passage be left to be performed by some other power, England, by her neglect of it, after having opened the East and West doors, would be laughed at by all the world for having hesitated to cross the threshold."

Sir John Barrow thought highly of Franklin and his leadership skills. Certainly Franklin had proven himself worthy on his previous Arctic expeditions, although he had lost nine men on the second one. On February 7, 1845, Franklin learned the good news. He was being sent north and west again, in command of two ships—the stalwarts of polar exploration, *Erebus* and *Terror*—with the express object of searching for and navigating through the Northwest Passage. The financial drawback to the command was that Franklin and his senior officers would draw only half pay while serving on the expedition, which could last as long as three years.

Enough was known about the Arctic west of Baffin Bay that the Admiralty's instructions to Franklin were clear. Get the two ships as far west through Lancaster Sound as possible, to 95°W if it could be attained. If that proved possible, the orders read, "From that point on we desire that every effort be used to penetrate to the southward and westward in a course as direct towards Bering Strait as the position and extent of the ice or existence of land at present unknown, may permit."

Although Franklin would to all appearances lead the expedition, he was to be little more than a figurehead. In almost every other way, the expedition was Sir John Barrow's project. Barrow chose the two ships, both of which had proven themselves capable of surviving the polar ice. Both were fitted with the most modern gadgetry, again on

Barrow's orders. Each ship was powered by a steam engine, as well as the traditional complement of sails. The engines, however, had not been designed for marine use; instead, they were converted railway engines of limited horsepower (25 hp for *Erebus* and only 20 hp for *Terror*). The two ships also had desalinization plants. Working to Barrow's plan, the Admiralty had retractable propellers installed on both ships. The Admiralty also looked after and paid for the victualling of the expedition, again according to Barrow's instructions.

Barrow also selected the officers, including the captains, of the two ships. James Fitzjames would be captain of *Erebus*, Franklin's flagship, and the highly experienced Irishman, Captain Francis Crozier, would be in command of *Terror*. Sixty-eight men would sail on *Erebus*, while a further 65 would handle *Terror*. Of the 133 men who embarked at Woolwich, 24 were officers, a somewhat higher percentage than should have been necessary. Extra to the crew were two dogs and a monkey.

A scant three months after Franklin's appointment, the two ships sailed from Woolwich with all men aboard and provisions for three years. Arctic veteran William Scoresby was convinced they had left too late in the season and would run into heavy ice. Subsequent events proved him right, but in the euphoria of the expedition's send-off, no one was listening. The two black-hulled ships, each decorated with a thick yellow stripe above the waterline and with gleaming white masts and yards, would have been a stirring sight as they moved down the Thames River.

With *Erebus* and *Terror* went two other naval ships, HMS *Baretto Junior* and HMS *Rattler*. The former was a supply ship and only intended to go with the convoy as far as the west coast of Greenland. *Rattler*, a steam frigate, and another vessel, *Monkey*, were ordered to escort the other three ships as far as the Orkney Islands and assist them in the first few days of their westbound voyage. Then they were to return home.

Erebus and *Terror*, both of which Franklin had visited in Hobart Town when they were en route to Antarctica in 1840, were the strongest navy ships available. Built from the best English oak, with thick hulls and enormous ribs and beams, they were beamy and had almost flat bottoms and bluff bows. As such, they were ideal for the anticipated trials of working through heavy ice. In addition, empty of their normal stocks of mortars and cannon shells, these "bomb" ships should have had a lot of storage space below decks for a long polar expedition, but the steam engines took up a considerable amount of room. While both ships had proven themselves in the Antarctic, *Terror* had also achieved distinction in the subarctic of Hudson Bay in 1836 by surviving a crushing blow from pack ice that threw her up onto an iceberg. Lieutenant George Back, who was in command at the time, not only got her back into her natural element without extra damage, he also sailed her home to the British Isles.

HMS *Erebus* was the larger of the two ships. She was 372 tons, and measured 105 feet (32 metres) in length and 29 feet (9 metres) across the beam. *Terror* was 13 years older than *Erebus* and weighed in at 326 tons. She was two feet (0.6 metres) shorter than *Erebus* and two feet narrower in the beam.

Sir John Barrow was taking no chances with these ships. History had demonstrated that Arctic ice had enormous destructive power. Accordingly, *Erebus* and *Terror* had 8-foot-thick (2.4-metre) wooden bows that were further strengthened and protected by sheet iron, one inch (2.5 centimetres) thick and stretching 20 feet (6 metres) on either side of the ship from the robust stem. The sides of the hulls consisted of five layers of wood fastened at different angles to a thickness of 10 inches (25 centimetres). The decks and bottoms were even stronger. The ships were, it was felt, indestructible. They were also much more comfortable than earlier polar-expedition vessels. The hulls were insulated with cork to keep out some of the cold. They had a central-heating system of steam pipes, and all hatches and doors were double the normal thickness.

The drawback to all the strengthening was that the already heavy ships, never good ocean sailors, were now so heavy that they waddled through the water rather than sprinted. However, there were advantages. Unlike previous ships, *Erebus* and *Terror* had what should have been reliable steam engines for propulsion and retractable propellers in place of paddlewheels. They would not be fast, but the Admiralty felt they would be safer than any ship before them. Their rudders, too, were an improvement over earlier designs. In the event the ships became trapped in ice, these new rudders could be detached in a few minutes and hauled out of harm's way. And both *Erebus* and *Terror* had enough lifeboats to carry everyone on board should they be forced to abandon ship at sea. If trapped in the ice and threatened with sinking, of course, the lifeboats would be useless.

Tens of tons of consumable stores, such as food, wine, beer and the ingredients for other drinks—tea, coffee, lime juice, etc.—had to be stowed away in the two hulls, along with 90 tons of coal for each ship to fire the steam boilers that ran the engines. Also on board, to record the expedition's activities, were cameras, some of the earliest ever made. Lady Franklin had added a gift for her husband: a silk Union Jack that she had stitched herself. Franklin's Arctic expedition of 1845 was the best-equipped force ever to be sent to the Arctic. It is understandable that Franklin was a proud and happy man as he set off, convinced the expedition would succeed.

At Stromness, *Monkey* was sent back to Woolwich and replaced by HMS *Blazer*. When the convoy left the Orkney Islands, *Rattler* and *Blazer* sailed with them as far as the vicinity of the rocky outcrop known as North Rona. There the two escorts came alongside the flagship, one to port and one to starboard. The crews of the two departing ships waved, gave three lusty cheers and turned for home. The Northwest Passage expedition continued west.

The Atlantic crossing from Scotland's Orkney Islands to Cape Farewell on the southern tip of Greenland was a slow one, taking four weeks and two days. At Disko Bay, on Greenland's west coast, the expedition loaded the additional coal and other supplies from *Baretto Junior*. In his final letter to Jane, Franklin reminded her that she and Eleanor should "not be too anxious, for it is very possible that our prospects of success and the health of our officers and men might justify our passing a second winter in these regions. If we do not succeed in our attempt, we shall try in other places."

With both ships now resupplied from the transport, on July 12, 1845, Franklin's expedition set sail for the northwest and the unknown. When *Baretto Junior* left Disko Bay soon after for England, she carried home four men who were deemed unfit for the rigours of the Arctic, plus the muster books from *Erebus* and *Terror* and official and personal letters. The four men who were sent home were the fortunate ones. The other 129 officers and men had already left to face the rigours of the Arctic.

Two hundred small copper cylinders were carried on board the flagship. They were to be used as containers for messages detailing the ships' locations and movements. These cylinders, which would float when sealed, were to be thrown overboard at regular intervals once the expedition passed 65° north latitude.

In Melville Bay, off the west coast of Greenland, two months after leaving England, Franklin's expedition met two whaling ships, *Prince of Wales* and *Enterprise*. The captains of those vessels later reported that Franklin's crews had been healthy and in good spirits. Captain Martin of *Enterprise* added that when he last saw Franklin's ships, they were anchored to a large ice floe in Baffin Bay and had set up an observatory on the highest point. They were also shooting hundreds of sea birds and salting them down to store for future consumption. It was the final visual communication the outside world had from the 129-strong Franklin expedition. Later, *Erebus* and *Terror* continued west into the ice of Lancaster Sound and were never seen again.

CHAPTER

9

Somewhere in the Arctic

THE ADMIRALTY'S ORDERS TO FRANKLIN, as issued by Sir John Barrow, may have been written in plain English, but the ice, not Admiralty orders, would decide the expedition's route. In fact, the orders were somewhat ambiguous and following them to the letter would have been all but impossible. The essence of the instructions, however, was to find a route through the Northwest Passage and follow it to the Bering Sea. The expedition should attempt to reach Cape Walker, on the northeastern part of Russell Island, just off the north coast of Prince of Wales Island. From there, the ships were to follow the most direct or convenient route to the west or southwest. But mere words on paper did not matter much when the ice dictated all movements.

Erebus and *Terror* are known to have sailed through Lancaster Sound as far as Barrow Strait. There they encountered ice too heavy for even those bull-nosed, steam-powered ships to force through, so Franklin turned his charges north into Wellington Channel, looking for open water. He failed to find a useable route but did successfully circumnavigate Cornwallis Island and returned to the ice of Barrow Strait, but he did not cross it to Cape Walker. With winter coming on fast, he had to find a safe haven in which to anchor the ships until the following open-water season, if it came.

Thanks to relics found at Cape Riley on the southwest corner of Devon Island and in a cairn on Beechey Island, we know that the expedition spent the winter of 1845–46 in the ice off bleak and desolate Beechey Island. Although blocked by heavy ice, the ships were out of the currents and protected by high cliffs. They would not need to be moved until breakup in the late spring. Moored within a short distance of each other, the two ships would have been connected by a trail across the ice marked with vertical stakes. Among the relics on Beechey Island were scattered a few hundred cans of food. Those unopened cans would one day answer a serious question about the expedition.

The winter would have been long and cold, but when the weather occasionally relented, the men could walk ashore on a marked route to stretch their legs, a small but important luxury. A storehouse and a smithy had been built ashore, which also gave them more room to move around on board. A large portion of the provisions that had crammed the ships and made them so uncomfortable went into safe storage on land for the duration of the sojourn in the ice. Even though the two ships were immovable in the icy bay, the sailors still had to work. They spent hours each day shovelling excess snow off the already insulated decks and stripping ice off the masts. Beyond that, the decks inside the ships had to be scrubbed constantly to keep them clean and as free of bacteria as possible.

Three deaths occurred that first winter, apparently of tuberculosis or scurvy. The men were buried on Beechey Island and markers erected over their graves. Autopsies performed on the bodies over a century later, in 1984, by Dr. Owen Beattie confirmed tuberculosis and pneumonia, but also revealed traces of lead poisoning in the body of seaman/stoker John Torrington.

As soon as the ice of Barrow Strait began to fracture and show signs of breaking up around the ships the following year, sailors reloaded the vessels and prepared for sea. They reinstalled and rigged the topmasts and yards, which had been stored for the winter, and replaced the sails. With the movement of the ice, the ships came alive again.

There were four routes available to Franklin from Beechey Island to the Beaufort Sea—if he could find them and, of course, if ice conditions permitted. He could have gone due south along the east coast of Somerset Island and through Bellot Strait to Franklin Strait, or he could have rounded the north end of Somerset Island and taken Peel Sound to Franklin Strait. A third option would have been to pass Cape Walker and follow the west side of Prince of Wales Island down McClintock Channel to the south end of Franklin Strait. He also could have attempted to sail due west into McClure Strait, the shortest and most direct course to the Beaufort Sea, but due to normal heavy ice concentration, that route was almost certainly not open to him.

It is most probable that *Erebus* and *Terror* followed one of the two routes to the south past Prince of Wales Island until they were beset by ice off the north or northwest coast of King William Island, between that piece of land and Gateshead Island. In late summer, under heavy ice conditions of the kind that Franklin would have encountered, Peel Sound should have offered the least resistance. The ice there would have been broken, in motion and of no great thickness. By contrast, the ice in McClintock Channel would have been much more concentrated and up to six feet (1.8 metres) thick.

Unfortunately for the expedition, and due to inaccurate mapping by earlier explorers, Franklin's charts would have shown King William Island marked as King William Land and attached to the North American mainland at the Boothia Peninsula. That extreme error meant that Franklin and his officers did not know there was a navigable passage down the east side of King William Island, or that it continued through

An aerial view of massive pieces of broken Arctic ice. Franklin's ships would have contended with far worse conditions than the ice congestion in this scene. ANTHONY DALTON

a narrow strait between the south side of that large island and the mainland, connecting to Queen Maud Gulf. Beyond that, through Coronation Gulf, named by Franklin in 1820, the waterway led almost due west to the open sea.

Assuming Franklin and his ice-navigation advisors had worked the ships down Peel Sound to a point close to the northwest shore of King William Island, they would have crunched into the much more compacted ice of the south end of McClintock Channel. Had they then continued to attempt to push south for the mainland, into what is now Victoria Strait, they would have found the ships surrounded by increasingly heavy ice. As the season advanced and the temperatures dropped, the ships became frozen in. They were trapped and had to prepare for another Arctic winter. This time, being well offshore, there would be no possibility of moving stores to the land.

Winter ice between King William Island, Prince of Wales Island and Victoria Island is a solid mass, dangerous in the extreme to a ship caught in its embrace. The ice is a confusion of blocks of all shapes and sizes littering the frozen sea. Worse, that ice is in motion, very slow motion to be sure, but in motion nonetheless. The ice is adrift on a weak current setting to the south, but that current can move ice mountains. As winter progresses, the frozen fields crack and raft up and over other ice. The rafting builds pressure ridges, sometimes as high as 100 feet (30 metres) above the surrounding fields. None of the icefields are smooth; most are a jumble of pale blue and white building blocks. Despite its enormous weight, as the ice moves with the current, it flexes and fractures. Its power is enormous. Ships can be crushed in minutes, and *Erebus* and *Terror* were no exception to that rule.

What would it have been like trapped in the ice, listening to it creaking and groaning and fracturing? Many years later, Captain Francis Leopold McClintock described it in his journal on October 28, 1857, while he was searching for evidence of Franklin in the Lady Franklin–sponsored luxury yacht *Fox*:

This evening, to our great astonishment, there occurred a disruption and movement of the ice within 200 yards of the ship. As I sit now in my cabin I can distinctly hear the ice crushing; it resembles the continued roar of distant surf, and there are many other occasional sounds; some of them remind me of the low moaning of the wind, others are loud and harsh, as if trains of heavy wagons with ungreased axles were slowly labouring along. Upon a less-favoured night these sounds might be appalling; even as it is, they are sufficiently ominous to invite reflection.

Once their ships had become trapped in the ice, the officers and men on board *Erebus* and *Terror* would have had to listen to the cacophony day and night for months at a time. They would never have been free of the fear that the next explosion of ice against ice might crush the two ships. Despite that fear, they had nowhere else to go. The world of ice outside the wooden hulls had become their prison.

CHAPTER

10

An Expedition Disappears

BY THE END OF 1846, with no word from the Franklin expedition or any sightings of the two ships or their crews, concerns for their welfare began to grow in England. Mitigating those concerns was the knowledge that John Ross and James Clark Ross and their crew had spent four winters in the ice between 1829 and 1833 on the paddle steamer *Victory* and lived to tell the tale. Therefore, it was believed, the Franklin expedition should not be in any grave danger, well equipped as it was for three or more years in the ice. But still, the Arctic was known to be a dangerous, unpredictable environment, so there was some doubt.

Sir John Ross had made Franklin a personal promise only two days before *Erebus* and *Terror* sailed from the

Thames River: "I shall volunteer to look for you, if you are not heard of in February 1847; but pray put a notice in the cairn where you winter, if you do proceed, [telling] which of the routes you take."

On February 9, 1847, Sir John Ross lived up to his word. He went to the Admiralty with his plans for a search-and-rescue mission, if that should be necessary, and was turned down. The august deciding body, made up of experts such as Barrow, Parry, Ross's estranged nephew, James Clark Ross, and Dr. Richardson, among others, all of whom should have known better, decided a relief expedition was unnecessary at that time. Old Sir John Ross was far from pleased at the apparent callousness of the decision and let his feelings be known in a strongly worded letter to the First Lord of the Admiralty. Again he was rejected and advised to talk to the Royal Society, as that association had been involved in the early arrangements for Franklin's expedition. The Royal Society turned Ross down, too, passing the responsibility back to the Admiralty.

Ross contacted Lady Franklin and was again disappointed. Jane had considerable faith in her missing husband and still believed he would win through. The months passed. Spring became summer and summer turned into autumn. As another winter approached, still there was no word of Franklin or his expedition. More people, in addition to Sir John Ross, began to show concern.

Early in November 1847, James Clark Ross approached

the Admiralty with plans for a relief expedition to search for Franklin, without telling his uncle of his intentions. Sir John Ross, ignorant of this activity, again contacted the Admiralty, only one week later than his nephew. John Ross's proposal was again rejected. His nephew's plan was accepted in December.

While the grey, wet winter continued in England, relief plans went into high gear. On January 30, 1848, HMS *Plover*, under the command of Captain Thomas Moore, was dispatched round the Horn to sail the length of the Pacific Ocean and through the Bering Strait to search for Franklin in the Beaufort Sea. Less than two months later, Dr. John Richardson and the HBC's Dr. John Rae left England. Their task would be to travel overland and on rivers across the muskeg and tundra to the Mackenzie River delta and follow the coast east to the mouth of the Coppermine River.

Sir James Clark Ross got under way on May 12, 1848, with two large naval ships, HMS *Enterprise* and HMS *Investigator*, planning to probe into the eastern Arctic and attempt to locate clues to Franklin's whereabouts. With Captain Edward Bird in charge of *Investigator* and Ross on the flagship, they were ably assisted by lieutenants Robert McClure and Leopold McClintock.

These three expeditions mounted in 1848, two by sea and one by land, were only the beginning of what would become the most complex and long-lasting search for missing explorers in history. The tireless and determined

Lady Franklin wanted to join the land expedition but was persuaded otherwise. Instead, she remained in England to raise money in case further rescue expeditions should be necessary, and she offered a reward of £2,000 for information regarding the missing ships.

HMS *Plover*, of course, went on her mammoth voyage for nothing. Her personnel found no trace of the expedition in the Bering Strait or Beaufort Sea area. Franklin had not gone through the passage. Richardson and Rae covered the coast far to the east and ascertained that the missing ships and crews had not reached the mainland. James Ross, however, spent a year in the Lancaster Sound/Somerset Island area and still missed the all-important evidence.

To be fair, *Enterprise* and *Investigator* had a difficult time in Greenland waters and in Baffin Bay due to ice. The two ships, therefore, did not enter Lancaster Sound until August 26, 1848, three years after Franklin disappeared. Ice buildup at the western end of Lancaster Sound was already heavy. Plans to search Wellington Channel, Barrow Strait and Prince Regent Inlet had to be abandoned for that season. On September 11, Ross moored his ships at Port Leopold on the northeast corner of North Somerset Island and prepared for a winter in the Arctic.

In the early spring of 1849, while the snow still covered the land and ice choked the waterways, Ross sent out sledging parties to build cairns at strategic locations in the hope that some of Franklin's men might be alive to find them. He also surveyed coastlines, adding information to maps and charts of the lands bordering Peel Sound. As an emergency measure, he had his men construct a house big enough for over 60 men on shore at Port Leopold and left a large cache of provisions there.

That year, the ice was late in breaking up, so the two ships were not able to break free of their harbour until August 29. They moved out into Barrow Strait with the intention of searching north and west but soon became caught up in the drifting ice surging into Lancaster Sound. Surrounded by pack ice with no way out, the ships were carried east into Baffin Bay before being set free. As it was then so late in the season, there was no point in attempting to regain lost ground. Ross turned his ships for home.

The relief expedition had failed to find Franklin or any signs of the lost expedition's whereabouts, but James Clark Ross had managed to accomplish some useful surveying work. He had also taught his two lieutenants the sledging skills they would need on future Arctic expeditions. Beyond that, others would have to continue the search.

Sir John Ross, 72 years old in the summer of 1849, continued to offer his considerable knowledge and skills to a search program. He advocated sending small ships, lightly manned. The Admiralty continued to turn him down. In a rather brilliant stroke of reasoning, Ross turned away from the Admiralty and approached the HBC. There he received a much more positive response to his plans.

The HBC agreed with the idea of smaller ships and offered their help. They handed over £500 toward the purchase of a ship. Additional amounts of £100 each came from other sources associated with the company. Sir Felix Booth, of gin fame, promised £1,000. Various other associates handed over small amounts. Ross was overjoyed and soon found a 91-ton schooner in Scotland. He named her *Felix*. Unfortunately for Ross, Booth died before handing over his donation, and after the expedition, Ross was never able to collect the money from the successor.

Wasting no time, Ross hired his officers and crew, making a total complement of 18 men with food supplies for 18 months. *Felix* sailed from Scotland one month short of Ross's 73rd birthday. It was a magnificent gesture for a man of Ross's age, as well as a serious venture. *Felix*, towing Ross's personal yacht *Mary*, arrived in Greenland just over three weeks later. The old sailor and explorer stayed there long enough to celebrate his birthday and hire an Inuit interpreter for the rest of the voyage.

The summer of 1850 was a busy time in the Canadian Arctic. In addition to Sir John Ross's expedition, there were at least five other groups searching for evidence of Franklin. Despite having turned Ross down, the Admiralty had sent three forces into the North. Four Royal Navy ships under the command of Captain Horatio Austin were in Lancaster Sound. Two more ships, *Lady Franklin* and *Sophia*, were in the same area and commanded by Captain

William Penny. Lady Franklin had sent out her own team, financed by herself and bolstered by public donations, in the 90-ton *Prince Albert* under Captain Charles Forsyth. That ship, too, was in the eastern Arctic. Joining that considerable search-and-rescue fleet were two more ships from America, *Advance* and *Rescue*, commanded by Captain E.J. de Haven, funded by Henry Grinnell, a wealthy New York businessman, and staffed by crews from the US Navy. The British Admiralty's third flotilla was sent through the Bering Strait to search the western Arctic. Again, those two ships were *Investigator* and *Enterprise*, captained by Robert McClure and Richard Collinson respectively.

None of the expeditions was successful in finding Franklin, although Penny was the first to find evidence of the winter sojourn in the ice off Beechey Island. In the west, *Investigator* and *Enterprise* became separated but explored on their own. Neither ship was successful in finding Franklin, but McClure, in *Investigator,* would complete a route through the Northwest Passage, albeit by abandoning his ship and walking on the fast ice to Barrow Strait and Beechey Island. But that was not until the summer of 1853.

11

Where is Franklin?

BACK IN ENGLAND, MAY 1850 brought with it disturbing news from a dead girl, no less. Not yet four years old when she died, Louisa Coppin, known to her family as Weasey, was said to visit her terrestrial family on a regular basis. The predictions she passed on to her siblings on those occasions usually happened. Some six weeks after she had correctly predicted the death of a local banker, Weasey was asked if she knew where Franklin might be. She replied through her sister, Anne, who told her listeners that Franklin and his ships were west of Prince Regent Inlet, near Point Victory off the northwest shore of King William Island. Weasey's father, Captain William Coppin, visited Lady Franklin and told her the story. She, in turn, told the captains of two separate expeditions she sent out. Neither of them took any apparent notice.

The search for Franklin's missing expedition was in high gear in the summer of 1850. An unprecedented concentration of would-be rescuers milled about in Arctic waters, the crews of each ship desperate to be the first to find evidence of any kind. The first clues to point to the Franklin expedition's voyage after it entered Lancaster Sound came to light when some of the rescue ships met there in August 1850. They were the transports for four separate relief expeditions. Captain de Haven from the Grinnell Expedition put men ashore at Cape Riley, at the southwestern corner of Devon Island, where Wellington Channel enters Barrow Strait, about the same time (August 23) that a party landed from *Intrepid*. Between them, they discovered obvious signs of a tent site, plus odds and ends of equipment, such as bits of canvas, rags, rope and broken bottles.

On August 25, while they were working to the west, lookouts on board *Rescue*, *Advance* and *Prince Albert* noticed two cairns on Cape Riley. The excitement was tempered by the subsequent discovery that the cairns were only two days old, having been built by American and British search parties. Meanwhile, lookouts on *Intrepid* spotted a cairn on a height of land on Beechey Island. A landing party tore it apart and inspected each and every stone without finding anything to suggest Franklin had been there. The following day, Captain William Penny arrived and went ashore to look at the cairns for himself. Although they yielded nothing, elsewhere he found substantial evidence that Franklin's expedition had spent time on Beechey Island.

Royal Navy lieutenant Sherard Osborn, serving as captain on board HMS *Pioneer*, wrote of visiting Beechey Island the next day. He described what they found:

> A multitude of preserved meat tins were strewed about, and near them and on the ridge of the slope a carefully constructed cairn was discovered; it consisted of layers of meat tins filled with gravel and placed to form a solid foundation; beyond this and along the northern shore of Beechey Island, the following traces were then quickly discovered—the embankment of a house with carpenter and armourer's working places, washing tubs, coal bags, pieces of old clothing, rope and lastly, the graves of three of the crew of *Erebus* and *Terror*—placing it beyond all doubt that the missing ships had indeed been there, and bearing the date of the winter of 1845–46.

The three names carved on the wooden markers were: W. Baines, a Royal Marine from *Erebus*, aged 32; Able Seaman John Hartnell, aged 25, also from *Erebus*; and John Torrington, a stoker, aged 20, from HMS *Terror*.

As the various parties roamed the island, they found deep marks made by sledge runners—British sledges, not Inuit. Osborn also noted some beer bottles, meat tins and odd bits of paper. Also among the clues were feathers and bits of fur, indicating the likelihood that birds and animals had been killed and eaten by Franklin's men.

While these finds excited the American and British seachers who scoured Beechey Island, Captain Forsyth of Lady Franklin's *Prince Albert* chose not to stay any longer in the Arctic. He headed east for home, where *Prince Albert* and its crew arrived early in October 1850 with little to show for the money spent, other than the second-hand news from Beechey Island. Lady Franklin was far from pleased and immediately began to organize a new expedition, once again using *Prince Albert* but with a different captain. The rest of the ships searching in the eastern Arctic that year spent the winter in the ice with the intention of resuming their activities in the spring and summer of 1851.

When the sledging season opened in April 1851, the sledge teams fanned out to search far and wide. Two parties, each with four sledges, made it to Cape Walker where it was believed Franklin would certainly have left a cairn containing information about his expedition's condition and detailing his planned movements from there. They were disappointed. The *Pilot of Arctic Canada*, the bible for navigating in Canadian Arctic waters, says of Cape Walker: "Along the shore at Cape Walker on Russel [sic] Island . . . the coast rises steeply to more than 800 feet." What is not said is that old ice from Viscount Melville Sound and Barrow Strait piles up in confused and chaotic mountains along the shores. The sledging parties, when they reached Cape Walker, found ice rafted up to 50 feet (15 metres) high in places. Their efforts in reaching the cape and in clambering over the unstable building blocks of ice were in vain. There was no cairn and no sign that any of Franklin's men had been there.

Once all the sledging parties had returned to their respective ships, without having found any more clues, the conclusion was that the lost expedition was nowhere near Cape Walker, nor within reach to the south or the west. Equally, the missing ships were not in or near Wellington Channel. The big questions that hung over the Arctic, which no one could answer, were quite simple: Where were *Erebus* and *Terror*? Where were the remaining 126 officers and men? And how could such a large expedition vanish without trace? Lady Franklin was determined to find the answers to those questions.

In 1851, crewmen on a naval ship in Baffin Bay claimed to have seen a large ice floe drifting south. Trapped on it were two black ships, each with a yellow stripe along the sides of the hull. The ships described matched the descriptions of *Erebus* and *Terror*. The navy ship is said to have trailed the ice floe until it and the ships sank. It is a romantic tale and an intriguing one, almost plausible but hardly credible.

When *Prince Albert* sailed away from Scotland for her second attempt at an Arctic rescue mission on June 3, 1851, Captain William Kennedy was in charge. Kennedy was part Cree and had known Sir John Franklin since Kennedy was a boy in Canada. Franklin had taught him to read and write.

Kennedy later worked the Labrador coast for eight years, distinguishing himself as a skilled sailor. His appointment to the command of *Prince Albert* came through his own persistence, after he had sailed to England at his own expense to offer his services to Lady Franklin. Second-in-command was a French naval officer, Lieutenant Joseph Bellot, who would give his name to the narrow strait that separates Somerset Island from the Boothia Peninsula.

Kennedy combed Prince Regent Inlet without success in the summer of 1851 and spent the winter in Batty Bay, on the east shore of Somerset Island. The rest of the ships searching the eastern Arctic had left for warmer waters in the early autumn of 1851. In the spring of 1852, Kennedy left his ship and most of his men in Batty Bay and travelled by dogsled for close to 1,400 miles (2,253 kilometres). He crossed Somerset Island and Peel Sound and reached as far west as Cape Walker before returning along the southern shore of Barrow Strait and down Prince Regent Inlet again to his iced-in ship. No results. At the end of the first week of August 1852, the ice released *Prince Albert* from Batty Bay, and Kennedy turned her for home. After the voyage, his written conclusions were that Franklin must have gone north to seek an ice-free route via Wellington Channel, Queen's Channel and then Penny Strait. Therefore he must be far to the west or north of where the main searches had been concentrated. Lady Franklin agreed with Kennedy. This gross error in direction was to be repeated by those who followed him.

By that time, the Admiralty had sent out another search-and-rescue fleet of five ships. *North Star*, a supply ship, went only to Beechey Island and was based there while the other ships went north and west. Two ships were to follow Wellington Channel while the other two attempted to reach Melville Island by sailing due west. The unpopular Sir Edward Belcher was 53 years old when he took command. His flagship was *Assistance*. Leopold McClintock was given *Intrepid*, Sherard Osborn took charge of *Pioneer* and Henry Kellett was on *Resolute*.

Assistance and *Pioneer* turned north after Beechey Island and pushed through Wellington Channel. They reached as far northwest as Northumberland Sound, at the northern end of Penny Strait, and settled in for the winter before the end of August 1852.

Intrepid and *Resolute* failed to reach Melville Island due to heavy ice and spent the winter at Dealy Island, close to the south side of Melville. And then, without warning, two expeditions came together. A sledge party, sent out to deposit food caches for the spring sledging season, found a message from Robert McClure at Winter Harbour on Melville Island. McClure had not been seen since he entered the Beaufort Sea from the Bering Strait in August 1850. The note said he was iced-in on Banks Island and gave co-ordinates for his ship. *Investigator* and *Resolute* were no more than 150 miles apart. When spring arrived, a sledging party from *Resolute* reached *Investigator*. Her crew members, most suffering from scurvy, were led east to the relative safety of the two ships at Dealy Island. Although Belcher's two-pronged expedition successfully rescued McClure and his men, and sledging parties from all four ships added vast amounts of knowledge to existing nautical charts, again, no trace of Franklin was found—because they were searching in the wrong area.

In England a few weeks later, the successes and failures of Belcher's expedition were overlooked as the news of McClure's discovery of the Northwest Passage route through what became known as McClure Strait was spread far and wide. The Northwest Passage, or one version of it, had been found, but the story of Belcher's expedition was far from over.

Early in 1854, with no sign of Franklin or any of his men for many years, they were officially given up for lost by the Admiralty. A handwritten note on the front page of the muster book for HMS *Erebus* reads, "Officers & ship's Co. are to be considered as having died in the service and their Wages are to be paid to their Relatives to 31 March 1854." With that brief notation, the Admiralty officially closed their records on the Franklin expedition. One hundred and twenty-six men had gone missing in the Arctic. For nine years their loved ones at home had waited and wondered. Those who relied solely on a husband or father's income for sustenance had lived for all those years without financial support. Now they received the back pay due to them, but there were still no concrete answers. What had happened to all those men and to the two ships?

The men on Belcher's flotilla had been unable to learn the answers. Now, in late August 1854, Belcher did the unthinkable. Against the entreaties of his senior officers, he abandoned his four main expedition ships to the Arctic ice. Belcher, his officers and men crowded aboard *North Star* and two other transports at Beechey Island and sailed for England. There, Belcher was court-martialled but acquitted. The Arctic, however, had more to say on the matter.

Resolute, one of the four abandoned ships, broke free of her icy prison and went on a voyage of her own. Unmanned, she navigated through 1,200 miles (1,930 kilometres) of waters littered with ice, including Lancaster Sound, Baffin Bay and Davis Strait, until she was sighted about 20 miles (32 kilometres) off Cape Mercy, on the southern tip of Baffin Island's Cumberland Peninsula, by a whaling ship in September the year after she was abandoned. Captain James Buddington of the American whaler *George Henry* towed the still manageable *Resolute* south to New London, Connecticut.

Once the families of the Franklin expedition's officers and crews had been paid off, the search was abandoned by the British and American authorities. However, someone else was out there in the Arctic in 1854. Renowned HBC explorer Dr. John Rae was on the west side of the Boothia Peninsula. In sight of the jumbled ice of a narrow strait he looked west and could just make out another land mass: King William Island. A local Inuit showed Rae a silver fork and spoon. Both had the initials F.R.M.C., scratched on them (rather than engraved). Rae had no idea who the initials represented, but they had to have been those of Captain Francis Rawdon Moira Crozier. But that was not all the Inuit would offer. They held even more treasures and had a tragic tale to tell of the fate of a large number of white men.

12

The Answers
Begin to Emerge

DR. JOHN RAE, WHO HAD been employed as a doctor and explorer for the HBC for years, was an expert in travelling and living Native style. On March 31, 1854, he left Repulse Bay planning to complete the maps of the north coast of mainland North America. By filling in the gaps, he expected to establish once and for all the existence of a southern route for the Northwest Passage.

Rae and four other men, two whites, one Inuit and one Cree, travelled long hours each day on snowshoes, pulling a heavy sledge, on a northwesterly route toward Pelly Bay. They then crossed the south side of Boothia Peninsula and reached the sea almost one month after leaving Repulse Bay.

On the way across Boothia, Rae encountered a large

party of Inuit. From them, he learned of the bodies of 35 to 40 white men who had starved to death an unspecified distance to the west, by a large river. But the information was too sketchy for Rae to consider exploring, so he continued his task of mapping the coast. On the northwest shores of Boothia he looked out over sea ice where his maps showed there should be land. In the distance he could see the land, but nothing in between. After making observations, Rae knew, without a doubt, that the land on the other side of the ice had to be King William—an island, not attached to Boothia. He might not have realized it at the time, but he had found the missing link in the Northwest Passage enigma.

Soon after Rae's return to Repulse Bay toward the end of May, he heard again from Inuit visitors of the men who had died of starvation somewhere to the west. They told him, through an interpreter, that about 40 men had been seen four years before. They were dragging sledges plus a boat on a sledge. Their description matched what Rae knew of the northwest side of King William Island. As the Inuit stories unfolded, it became obvious that some of the white men, at least, had managed to reach the south side of King William Island and had crossed to the mouth of Back's Fish River, where their camp and dead bodies were found on Montreal Island in the river's mouth.

From the Inuit's description of the state of some of the bodies, it became clear to Rae that the white men had resorted to cannibalism to stay alive—for a while. The Inuit also traded relics found with the bodies; Rae recorded a total of 15 pieces, many bearing identifying marks that pointed to the lost Franklin expedition. As soon as possible, Rae returned to England to report the news to the Admiralty and to the general public.

An incensed Lady Franklin refused to believe Rae's cannibalism story and accused him of damaging her missing husband's good name. She began lobbying for an expedition to verify or vilify Rae's shocking report, preferably the latter. In conjunction with the HBC, the Admiralty arranged for an experienced HBC trader, recommended by Rae, to look at the sites the Inuit people had mentioned. James Anderson was commissioned to lead a survey party down Back's Fish River to the north coast and look into the story. He left Fort Resolution on June 20, 1855, and returned on September 17. His river journey to Montreal Island corroborated Rae's story, as told by the Inuit. Lady Franklin was still not satisfied. She sent out another expedition.

William Hobson, a Royal Navy lieutenant serving on board the steam-schooner *Fox*, sent to the Arctic in 1857 by Lady Franklin and commanded by Captain Leopold McClintock, was the first to find even more important but tragic clues to the disappearance of the expedition. While *Fox* was in winter quarters at Port Kennedy, at the eastern end of Bellot Strait, McClintock took a sledging party southeast toward the site of the north magnetic pole, where he hoped to meet Natives. They came to a camp where 45 or more Inuit showed them items for trade: silver forks and spoons, as well as naval buttons and other items that could only have come from a ship. The Inuit said they had heard about a ship that had been crushed in the ice off King William Island. All the men on board, they said, had landed ashore safely. They had found the cutlery and other relics, they explained, in a different direction, on an island in a river. McClintock recognized that this information corresponded to the story Rae had been told. McClintock went back to his ship and laid plans for two major sledging expeditions early in the spring.

When the weather improved enough for sledging, two parties left *Fox*. They travelled together down the west coast of Boothia Peninsula to Cape Victoria, not far from the north magnetic pole site, and just 25 miles (40 kilometres) across James Ross Strait from King William Island. En route they met Inuit who told them of two ships that had been trapped in ice off King William Island. One had been crushed and sunk. The other had fetched up on shore. The stories were hearsay, nothing more. None of the Inuit claimed to have been there. They said the tales they heard had spoken of Inuit going on board the on-shore wreck and finding the remains of a very large man with long teeth. They further explained that the stories said the white men had gone south to a large river and that they had a boat, or boats, with them.

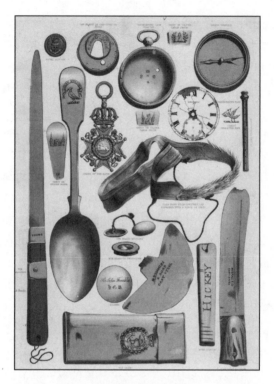

Relics of the Franklin expedition, including various knives, a spoon, Franklin's Order of the Bath medal, parts of a chronometer, a hatband from an officer's cap (repaired with animal skin), a small tin box and brass buttons.

The news must have excited McClintock, but he was not prepared to rush blindly to search for a ship and men based on vague, second-hand stories from a few years before. He continued with his plans. McClintock sent Hobson and his team to the northern part of King William Island. In the meantime, he and another sledging party explored a southern route as far as Chantrey Inlet, which was, in effect, the vast mouth of Back's Fish River. On Montreal Island in Chantrey Inlet, McClintock found some pieces of iron and wood but little more. He crossed over Simpson Strait to King William Island and moved west along the coast, where he found a skeleton. He also found some clothing remnants, a hair comb and brush, plus a frozen pocket book. The clothing belonged to one of Franklin's men—Henry Peglar, an officer's steward.

On May 5, 1859, during his sledging journey along the northwest shores of King William Island with other sailors, some 200 miles (320 kilometres) from *Fox*, Lieutenant Hobson found a cairn of stones, as tall as a large man. The cairn was surrounded by an untidy pile of discarded European clothing, plus mattresses and blankets. Close by stood cooking utensils, carpenter's tools and other ship's paraphernalia.

Hobson, suffering terribly from scurvy but still alert, could not believe his eyes. Using what little strength he had left, he tore open the cairn. Inside he found a cylinder— the only one of the 200 cylinders carried on board ever to be found. It had been sealed with lead but later broken open. Inside he found a message on Admiralty paper requesting that the single sheet be forwarded to the Secretary of the

Admiralty in London. Handwritten around the central theme were two other messages. One reported on the winter of 1846–47:

> 28 of May 1847. HM Ships *Erebus* and *Terror* wintered in the ice in Lat. 70°-05′N. Long. 98°-23′W. Having wintered in 1846–47 at Beechey Island in Lat. 74°-43′-28″N. Long. 90°-39′- 15″W., after having ascended Wellington Channel to Lat. 77°, and returned by the west side of Cornwallis Island. Sir John Franklin commanding the expedition. All well. Party consisting of 2 officers and 6 men left the ships on Monday 24th May 1847. –Gm. Gore, Lieut, Chas. F. DesVoeux, Mate.

There is an obvious error here. The ships actually wintered on Beechey Island over the dark months of 1845–46, not 1846–47. So far so good, but the second message held tragic news:

> April 25, 1848—HM's ships *Terror* and *Erebus* were deserted on 22nd April, 5 leagues N.N.W. of this, having been beset since 12th September 1846. The officers and crews, consisting of 105 souls, under the command of Captain F.R.M. Crozier, landed here in Lat. 69°-37′42″N., long. 98°-41″W . . . Sir John Franklin died on 11th June 1847; the total loss by deaths in the Expedition has been to this date 9 officers and 15 men.
>
> James Fitzjames, Captain HMS *Erebus*
> F.R.M. Crozier, Captain and Senior Officer
>
> And start tomorrow, 26th, for Back's Fish River.

The locations given for the ships corresponded with the information given by the late Weasey Coppin nine years earlier. Lieutenant Hobson may or may not have known that surreal tale. What he did now know was that Sir John Franklin and 23 of his officers and men had died more than 11 years before. Other than the few graves on Beechey Island, no trace had been found of other associated burial sites. Almost certainly, given the naval tradition, Sir John's emaciated body would have been dressed in his best uniform, wrapped in a Union Jack (probably the silk one made for him by Lady Franklin), weighted with lead and buried at sea. To achieve that end, sailors would have had to cut or burn a hole in the ice.

With so many dead, far more than on any other British Arctic expedition, and no sign of any survivors for over a decade, it was obvious to Hobson that the rest of the officers and crew must also have perished somewhere between the cairn and the stated destination of Back's Fish River (now called Back River) on the mainland, hundreds of miles across inhospitable terrain to the south. There was one unspoken question: How far could the survivors have walked before exhaustion, lack of food and the dreadful cold sapped their physical and mental strength? Hobson and his men continued southwest along the coast for six days until he saw a startling sight in the distance.

Standing alone on an oaken sledge was what appeared to be a boat. When he came closer, Hobson knew from its design that the boat could only have come from one of the missing ships. When he looked over the gunwales, the scene inside the boat filled him with horror. There were two human skeletons. One was fully dressed, covered in furs and seated in the stern. Beside it, close to the left hand, was a loaded and primed shotgun. Another shotgun, in similar condition, was close to the right hand. The other skeleton was nothing more than a disorderly pile of mangled and partly eaten bones in the bow.

Between the two, looking from bow to stern, were a pair of slippers, five bibles and one novel, soap and towels, silk handkerchiefs and eight pairs of boots. Two rolls of sheet lead lay against the port side of the hull. There were brushes and combs, knives, saws and other carpenter's tools, a pile of wool clothing, powder and shot, 40 pounds (18 kilograms) of chocolate, and perhaps the most telling of all, five gold watches and 26 pieces of silver cutlery. Each piece of silverware carried the personal crest of either Franklin or one of his officers. To add to the sad tableau was another mystery: the sledge and boat were facing toward the northeast, not to the south as would have been expected for sailors trying to reach Back's Fish River.

Although Hobson never expressed the thought out loud or on paper, the scene in front of him told its own appalling tale. The unknown figure seated in the stern with the shotgun had probably murdered and then eaten his fellow sailor in the bow.

The snow was thick underfoot and fog swirled around them. Hobson and his men were in great danger themselves from the cold, hunger and scurvy. Having finally uncovered concrete evidence of the Franklin expedition, Hobson left the bizarre tableau as he had found it and continued down the coast as far as Erebus Bay. There he built a cairn and left a message for McClintock. Hobson then fought his way back to *Fox*.

When Hobson and his men left the stranded boat, they had been unaware that there was more evidence of cannibalism buried under the snow at their feet. Those grisly pieces of history would have to wait for another time.

McClintock found Hobson's cairn and note and continued his trek to see the terrible scene for himself. He retraced Hobson's route to the boat on the sledge, to the cairn and so back to *Fox*. There was no longer any doubt about the fate of Franklin and the crews of his two ships. All that was left was for McClintock to return to England, which he did in September 1859, and tell Lady Franklin the tragic news of the complete loss of the largest expedition ever to work in the Arctic.

Epilogue

IN MAY 1860, LADY FRANKLIN was delighted to receive the Royal Geographical Society's Founders' Gold Medal. It was awarded to acknowledge Sir John Franklin's discovery of the Northwest Passage. To her, and to her close relatives, it was a fitting epitaph for her long-dead husband.

The Gold Medal was a well-deserved honour, but unfortunately, in the last few decades, Sir John Franklin has not been dealt with kindly by many writers, often being depicted as a bumbling failure. There is no doubt that he sometimes failed, but most of the time he was just plain unlucky. The North Pole expedition of 1818 has been cited as an example of his incompetence, but he was not the man in charge. His first overland journey to the Arctic lost nine men, mostly due to starvation. Those tragic deaths went against Franklin's record, but during that expedition he charted the courses of rivers and filled in significant gaps in maps of the Arctic coastline, coming close to solving the riddle of the Northwest Passage. His second overland expedition added much more to Britain's knowledge of the Arctic coast west of the Mackenzie River. Franklin's six-year sojourn as governor of Van Diemen's Land could not be judged a success; clearly, he was not a politician. Franklin's final expedition, a huge undertaking for the time, was planned and organized by Sir John Barrow. Sir John Franklin was the figurehead and leader; as far as we know, he proved his worth in that capacity. Although the expedition was lost in the Arctic ice, Franklin did achieve part of the expedition's goals: he discovered one of the routes through the Northwest Passage.

Sir John Franklin was popular with most of his officers and men while at sea and on his arduous overland journeys. He was articulate and kind, a skilled navigator and fearless of personal danger. When his accomplishments and character are all considered, he should be remembered as a fine man, a determined leader and an explorer worthy of the name.

In the two or three decades following McClintock's grim news in 1859, occasional expeditions studied the known sites on King William Island. None found anything new until the early 1930s, when pilot Walter Gilbert saw a few artifacts from the Franklin expedition on the northwest coast of King William Island. A year later, William Gibson of the HBC located more human bones and artifacts on the south shore of the island. In 1993, a team of explorers and archaeologists from Canada returned to the boat on the northwest shores of King William Island. Under the surrounding snow, they found more grisly evidence of what had befallen at least some of Franklin's men. Around the boat and its sledge cradle were the remains of 14 other men. These once strong men, or their remains, had not fallen victim to marauding polar bears or other animal predators. The bones showed clear signs that the flesh had been carved off with knives.

Other traces of the lost expedition have been found, some considerably farther south. But no signs have ever been found of the two ships, other than scraps of wood picked up by Inuit. Franklin's final note, as placed in the cairn by Lieutenant Gore, was explicit as to the location of the two vessels just before he died. That position placed them 23 miles (37 kilometres) from shore. The second note, left by Crozier a little less than a year later, did not give precise coordinates for the ships. Instead, it stated that the ships were abandoned five leagues north-northwest of the cairn. A league can represent anywhere from two and a half to four and a half miles (four to seven kilometres). Therefore, five leagues equates to somewhere roughly between 12 and 22 miles (20 and 36 kilometres) from the cairn. That would have placed them close to the confluence

Epilogue

The skulls of some of Franklin's missing men were found on King William Island. LIBRARY AND ARCHIVES CANADA PA-147732

of today's McClintock Channel, Franklin Strait, Victoria Strait and James Ross Strait—certainly, at the farthest extremity, not far from the coordinates given by Franklin. It is possible that the ships had drifted closer to the shores of King William Island with the slow current.

Arctic ice, however, moves in relentless fashion with the seasons. The ships could have been crushed where they were last seen, or they could have been carried away, separately or together, to drift with the ice for hundreds of miles before the relentless pressure consumed them. Their shattered timbers could rest anywhere.

In 1992, the still unknown site of Franklin's ships was named HMS Erebus and HMS Terror National Historic Site of Canada. Beginning in 2008, Parks Canada's Underwater Archaeological Service embarked on a three-year expedition to determine the locations of Franklin's ships. Working in collaboration with the Canadian Hydrographic Service, the Canadian Coast Guard and the Government of Nunavut, in 2008 and 2010, the expedition surveyed over 77 square miles (200 square kilometres) of water north of King William Island. The surveys continued in 2011, this time with the additional collaboration of the University of Victoria's Ocean Technology Laboratory and the Canadian Ice Service. Although results to date have failed to find the ships, the search will continue.

In the summer of 2010, a Parks Canada expedition discovered the wreck of McClure's HMS *Investigator* in Mercy Bay on the north side of Banks Island. That important find has renewed interest in the possibility of eventually discovering the remains of either HMS *Erebus* or HMS *Terror*.

The last resting place of Sir John Franklin is as much a mystery as the location of the two ships he so ably commanded. After sliding through a hole in the ice cut by his shipmates in June 1847, the great explorer's weighted body, draped in the Union Jack, settled to the sea bed, there to reside for eternity. There is no record of the latitude and longitude of the burial site.

In addition to the location of the ships, there was another important question. Why did so many officers and men die before abandoning the ships when there should still have been so much food available on board? Perhaps the answer to that question was closer to home. Admiralty records show that the Franklin expedition was supplied with canned food by Goldner's of Houndsditch, in east London. These were the cans found on Beechey Island many years later. Modern analysis of the cans' construction and contents has revealed some stark and horrifying truths. The cans were substandard and almost certainly caused lead poisoning in those who ate from them. While not necessarily fatal, the ingestion of lead would certainly have created severe medical problems for a crew of men who needed to be able to work hard to keep the expedition on course. Most significant of those medical problems would have been chronic fatigue and lethargy. In addition to lead, the contents of the cans, supposedly meat in some and vegetables in others, were found to have significant traces of *Clostridium botulinum*, which causes botulism, still a serious disease in the modern world. In the 19th-century Arctic, with limited medical facilities or drugs on the ships, botulism would have usually proved fatal. Botulism shows its presence early, anywhere from a few hours to a day or two after the toxin is ingested, with gastrointestinal problems including nausea and stomach cramps. These are followed by neurological disorders. Muscle weakness gives way to paralysis and can lead to respiratory failure. If untreated, sufferers can die within three days of exhibiting the first symptoms.

The most important players in 19th-century Arctic exploration faded one by one into history in the years following Franklin's disappearance. Sir John Barrow died in November 1848. Sir John Ross followed him in London in 1856, and Sir James Clark Ross in 1862. Dr. John Richardson hung on until 1865. Lady Jane Franklin passed away ten years later in 1875 at the age of 83. Sir George Back went on to achieve fame as an admiral and as president of the Royal Geographical Society, which he served for over 20 years. He was never popular but appeared to be oblivious of that fact. He died in June 1878. Dr. John Rae lasted until July 1893, when he died of pneumonia in London. Francis Crozier, one of the most experienced of polar explorers, left his bones somewhere on the horrific foot-slog from the northwest shore of King William Island to the mouth of Back's Fish River, presumably sometime in late 1848 or early 1849.

Sixty years after the Franklin expedition disappeared, the consummate Norwegian explorer Roald Amundsen and a crew of six took a 70-foot-long (21-metre) herring boat, *Gjoa*, from east to west through the Northwest Passage between 1903 and 1906 using the southern route through Dolphin and Union Strait, Queen Maud Gulf and Rae Strait.

Epilogue

This first successful transit was led by a man who, as a boy, had considered Sir John Franklin his hero. Even then, no one knew the full story of what had happened to the Franklin expedition. Most of that complicated riddle was not solved until the late 20th century.

Dutch-Belgian long-distance sailor Willi de Roos was the first small-boat skipper to complete a transit of the Northwest Passage. He sailed from east to west in the 43-foot (13-metre) steel ketch *Williwaw* in 1977. The author of this book failed in a solo attempt on the passage from west to east in *Audacity*, a small powerboat, in 1984. Since then many others have attempted the passage—some failed; some won through. In more recent years, the Arctic ice has melted enough each summer that more and more small vessels have been able to transit the passage in one season.

The ice continues to freeze the Northwest Passage in winter. In the short northern summer it releases its grip and allows intruders to explore its difficult coastlines. Yet no matter how many adventurers challenge the historic passage, it is unlikely that any will achieve the fame of the expedition led by the Lion of the Arctic. Today, 167 years after *Erebus* and *Terror* vanished in the Arctic seas, the fascination with the fate of Franklin, his officers and men, as well as the two ships, continues unabated.

Selected Bibliography

Beattie, Owen and John Geiger. *Frozen in Time: Unlocking the Secrets of the Lost Franklin Expedition.* 3rd ed. Vancouver: Douglas & McIntyre, 2004.

Berton, Pierre. *The Arctic Grail: The Quest for the North West Passage and the North Pole, 1818–1909.* Toronto: McClelland & Stewart, 1988.

Cookman, Scott. *Ice Blink: The Tragic Fate of Sir John Franklin's Lost Polar Expedition.* New York: Wiley, 2000.

Cyriax, Richard. *Sir John Franklin's Last Expedition.* London: Methuen, 1939.

Dalton, Anthony. *Alone against the Arctic.* Victoria: Heritage House, 2006.

———. *River Rough, River Smooth.* Toronto: Natural Heritage/Dundurn, 2010.

Dodge, Ernest S. *The Polar Rosses.* London: Faber & Faber, 1973.

Fleming, Fergus. *Barrow's Boys: The Original Extreme Adventurers.* New York: Atlantic Monthly Press, 1998.

Franklin, Sir John. *Narrative of a Journey to the Shores of the Polar Sea in the years 1819-20-21-22.* London: John Murray, 1823.

———. *Narrative of a Second Expedition to the Shores of the Polar Sea in the years 1825, 1826, and 1827.* London: John Murray, 1828.

Hood, Robert and Stuart C. Houston, eds. *To the Arctic by Canoe, 1819–1821.* Montreal: McGill-Queen's, 1974.

LaFleur, Claude, ed. *Pilot of Arctic Canada.* Vol. 1. 2nd ed. Ottawa: Canadian Hydrographic Service, 1970.

Selected Bibliography

Latta, Jeffrey Blair. *The Franklin Conspiracy*. Toronto: Dundurn, 2001.

MacDonald, John. *The Franklin Trail*. http://www.netscapades.com/franklintrail/

MacInnis, Joe. *The Breadalbane Adventure*. Montreal: Optimum, 1982.

McClure, Robert Le M. *The Discovery of the North-West Passage*. Rutland, VT: Charles E.Tuttle Co., 1969.

McGoogan, Ken. *Fatal Passage*. Toronto: HarperCollins, 2001.

Mountfield, David. *A History of Polar Exploration*. New York: Dial Press, 1974.

Mowat, Farley. *Ordeal by Ice*. Toronto: McClelland and Stewart, 1960.

Owen, Roderick. *The Fate of Franklin*. London: Hutchinson, 1978.

Thompson, George Malcolm. *The Search for the North-West Passage*. New York: Macmillan, 1975.

Index

Index

Acknowledgements

As always, I wish to acknowledge the exceptional team at Heritage House for their ongoing support. Between them they turn my words into beautiful books. Thank you to publisher Rodger Touchie, managing editor Vivian Sinclair, my exceptional editor Lesley Reynolds, marketing specialist Neil Wedin, proofreaders Karla Decker and Liesbeth Leatherbarrow, production manager Susan Adamson, designers Chyla Cardinal, Francis Hunter and Jacqui Thomas, plus all the friendly and efficient staff at the Heritage Group distribution centre in Surrey, BC. You have my admiration for your ever cheerful professionalism.

Many thanks to Jill Butcher, my long-time, long-distance friend and fellow writer, who encouraged me to finish this book when I faltered, and to my pal of more than three decades, Steve Crowhurst, for his unfailing enthusiasm for all my projects—literary, adventure and nautical.

The Canadian Authors Association has played a large role in my life for almost a decade. I am indebted to many of my fellow members for their support and friendship. They know who they are.

I am honoured to be a Fellow of the Royal Geographical Society, as was Sir John Franklin. Formed in London in 1830, that august body and its distinguished members have played significant roles in expeditions all over the world, including many in the Arctic regions.

About the Author

Anthony Dalton is the author of 12 non-fiction books and co-author of 2 others, many of which are about the sea, ships or his own adventures in small boats and on land. These include *Fire Canoes*; *The Fur-Trade Fleet*; *Polar Bears*; *A Long, Dangerous Coastline*; *The Graveyard of the Pacific*; *Alone Against the Arctic*; and *Baychimo: Arctic Ghost Ship*, all published by Heritage House. As a freelance writer and photographer, magazine assignments have taken him over much of the world. A former expedition organizer and leader working in the Sahara, the deserts of the Middle East and occasionally in the Arctic, he is a Fellow of the Royal Geographical Society (FRGS), a Fellow of the Explorers Club and past president of the Canadian Authors Association. In recent years he has received many awards and honours, including a listing in the 100th anniversary edition of *Canadian Who's Who*. Since the fall of 2011, Anthony has been travelling the world as a featured guest speaker on a variety of ships for two cruise lines. When he's not travelling, he lives in the lower mainland of British Columbia.

Anthony Dalton is also the author of *Wayward Sailor: In Search of the Real Tristan Jones*; *J/Boats: Sailing to Success*; *Adventures with Camera and Pen*; *River Rough, River Smooth*; and *Arctic Naturalist: The Life of J. Dewey Soper*.

More Amazing Stories by Anthony Dalton

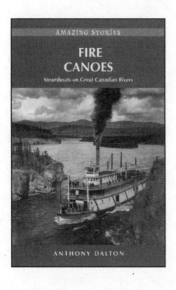

Fire Canoes

Steamboats on
Great Canadian Rivers

print ISBN 978-1-927051-45-0
ebook ISBN 978-1-927051-46-7

Anson Northup, the first steamboat on the Canadian prairies, arrived in Fort Garry in 1859. Belching hot sparks and growling in fury, it was called "fire canoe" by the local Cree. For 150 years, steamboats carried passengers and freight on the greatest—and most dangerous—Canadian rivers, leaving behind tales of flamboyance and daring that coloured the history of this country. Travel back in time aboard gold-rush paddle-steamers on the Yukon River, rugged sternwheelers on the Saskatchewan and Red Rivers and luxurious liners on the St. Lawrence to the decades when steamboats sent the echoes of their shrill whistles across this vast land.

Visit heritagehouse.ca to see the entire list of books in the Amazing Stories series.

More Amazing Stories by Anthony Dalton

The Graveyard of the Pacific
Shipwreck Tales from the Depths of History

print ISBN 978-1-926613-31-4
ebook ISBN 978-1-926936-31-4

The magnificent west coast of Vancouver Island is renowned for its rugged splendour, but the coastline known as the Graveyard of the Pacific is haunted by the ghosts of doomed ships and long-dead mariners. These true tales of disastrous shipwrecks and daring rescues are a fascinating adventure into West Coast maritime history.

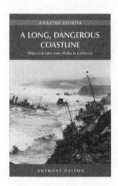

A Long, Dangerous Coastline
Shipwreck Tales from Alaska to California

print ISBN 978-1-926613-73-4
ebook ISBN 978-1-926936-11-6

From San Francisco's Golden Gate to the Inside Passage of British Columbia and Alaska, the west coast of North America has taken a deadly toll. Here are the dramatic tales of ships that met their end on this treacherous coastline—including *Princess Sophia*, *Queen of the North* and others— and the tragic stories of those who sailed aboard them.

Visit heritagehouse.ca to see the entire list of books in the Amazing Stories series.

More Amazing Stories by Anthony Dalton

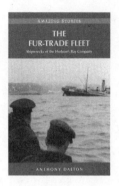

The Fur-Trade Fleet
Shipwrecks of the Hudson's Bay Company

print ISBN 978-1-926936-09-3
ebook ISBN 978-1-926936-07-9

Since the 17th century, hundreds of ships have sailed in the Hudson's Bay Company's fur-trade fleet, servicing far-flung northern posts and braving the wild rapids of mighty rivers. During these arduous voyages, many of these ships and their courageous crews came to grief. Here are the dramatic stories of the legendary ships that proudly flew the flag of Canada's oldest company.

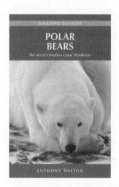

Polar Bears
The Arctic's Fearless Great Wanderers

print ISBN 978-1-926613-74-1
ebook ISBN 978-1-926936-25-3

Polar bears have become a charismatic symbol of animals threatened by climate change, yet in the past they were feared and hunted indiscriminately by Arctic adventurers. These fascinating stories draw from the annals of northern exploration and more recent polar bear research to capture the power and majesty of the world's largest land carnivore.

Visit heritagehouse.ca to see the entire list of books in the Amazing Stories series.